International Strategic Alliances

Co-operating to Compete

International Strategic Alliances

Co-operating to Compete

David Faulkner

McGRAW-HILL BOOK COMPANY

London · New York · St Louis · San Francisco · Auckland
Bogotá · Caracas · Lisbon · Madrid · Mexico · Milan
Montreal · New Delhi · Panama · Paris · San Juan · São Paulo
Singapore · Sydney · Tokyo · Toronto

Published by
McGRAW-HILL Book Company Europe
Shoppenhangers Road, Maidenhead, Berkshire, SL6 2QL, England
Telephone 0628 23432
Fax 0628 770224

British Library Cataloguing in Publication Data
Faulkner, David
  International Strategic Alliances:
  Co-operating to Compete
  I. Title
  658.16
  ISBN 0–07–707926–4

Library of Congress Cataloging-in-Publication Data
Faulkner, David
      International strategic alliances: co-operating to compete/David
  Faulkner.
    p. cm.
    Includes bibliographical references and index.
    ISBN 0–07–707926–4
    1. Strategic alliances (Business) – Case studies. 2. International
  business enterprises – Case studies. I. Title
  HD69.S8F38   1995   94–29589
  338.8'8–dc10   CIP

12345   BL   998765

Typeset by Computape (Pickering) Ltd., North Yorkshire
and printed and bound in Great Britain by Biddles Ltd, Guildford, Surrey.

Contents

Preface

From 1986 onwards I discovered, in my then profession of strategic management consultant, that an ever-increasing number of clients were approaching me with projects in which they were seeking partners in other countries in preparation for the arrival of the single European market in 1992. In order to serve them satisfactorily I began to scan the management literature for answers to such questions as:

- How do I set up a strategic alliance?
- What are the various forms of alliance, and in what circumstances is each of them most appropriate?
- What are the basic rules for managing alliances successfully?
- What qualities should I seek in a partner?

I was surprised to find that the subject was very inadequately covered in the management literature. Generally, commentary in the area was confined to articles in journals, or small parts of books on multinationals, and the consensus seemed to be that alliances were transitory inter-organizational devices, adopted by weaker companies to cover projects they felt inadequately resourced to tackle alone. I therefore decided to set up a research project to seek to answer the key questions on alliances by investigating a substantial number of cross-border alliances currently in operation.

Since that time I have become a management academic at Cranfield University's School of Management (although I have still maintained involvement in the strategic consulting world) and the alliance research has served to provide me with the data for the doctoral thesis necessary to gain respectability in the academic world. At the same time, the areas of international strategic alliances has been dramatically transformed into a 'hot' subject, and the number of scholars and practitioners interested in the subject has multiplied greatly. Now, instead of being a 'second-best solution', the strategic alliance is seen as the inter-organizational form of the future for all firms facing the need to operate and survive in a global market.

This book, which analyses and draws lessons from 67 international alliances, may well be timely. It deals with general lessons deducible from the analysis of questionnaires completed by executives involved in the 67 alliances, and supplements these general lessons with case histories of nine alliances in such a way that the histories consider in contextual detail similar questions to those contained in the questionnaires, but with the advantage of providing specific and historical perspective.

The book is intended to be accessible to the interested businessperson in particular, who may well be considering setting up alliances with continental or other partners. It is based on academic research, however, and may therefore also be of interest to students and colleagues.

David Faulkner
1994

Acknowledgements

I should like to acknowledge the co-operation of all the executives who provided the perceptual data in the questionnaires, and gave so willingly of their time to enable me to develop the case studies. Without their assistance the four-year project could never have been carried out. In management research, access is in many ways the key, and in this respect I have been very fortunate. The majority of the research was conducted during 1992 and 1993.

1 The growth of co-operation

The international strategic alliance is currently a fast-growing inter-organizational form that has gained increasing popularity over the last few years. There are a number of possible reasons for this. First, the economic world is developing into a group of larger trading blocs with lower tariff levels and dramatically reduced transmission times for products and information. Second, there is an increasing globalization of markets in an ever-widening band of industries, together with the development of global technologies that shorten production cycles, and an ever-increasing demand for investment resources to cope with the changing environment.

A major data-collection exercise at INSEAD on the formation of international strategic alliances confirms the accelerating growth of all forms of strategic alliance, as does UK research, which suggests that Europe has been the area of fastest growth in recent years (see Figure 1.1).

It is noticeable that the prime motor for growth since 1986 appears to have been among firms within the European Community (EC).

ALLIANCE DEVELOPMENT

The process of economic and industrial change in the West since the end of the Second World War can be characterized by a number of phases, as Professor Chandler explains in his book *Scale and Scope: The Dynamics of Industrial Capitalism* (1990). First there was the immediate post-war phase of inherited rigidities from the inter-war period, and the

1

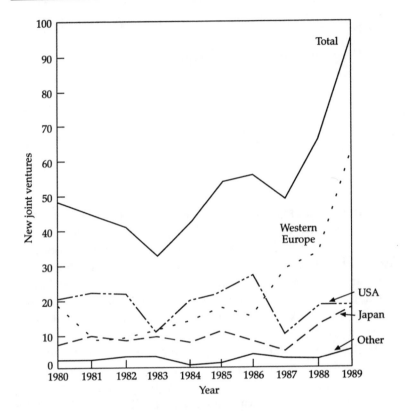

Figure 1.1 UK joint venture formation region by year: 1980–89 (*source:* Glaister and Buckley, 1994)

protection of economies ravaged by war. Then, from the 1950s onwards, came the dramatic growth of the major multinationals and of the multi-divisionalized form (M-form) of organization. The M-form of company organization became the dominant means of coordinating the sale and delivery of goods to customers. The market mechanism was in effect replaced by an internal administrative system within, rather than outside the company.

However, this eventually led to administrative and bureaucratic diseconomies that had to be weighed against the realization of the clear scale and scope economies of large-scale operation. A weakening of market discipline led to the growth of inflexibility, corporate arrogance, diminished speed of response to markets and a lessened free flow of information within the companies intent on implementing global strategies.

The third phase came in the late 1970s and 1980s when the system began to change its nature in response to the pressure resulting from these inflexibilities. This period saw the growth of the venture capital-funded entrepreneurial firm with substantial outsourcing of non-key processes. Thus, activities that had previously been performed within the company were returned to the marketplace. This, of course, showed in many instances the disadvantage of fragmentation and the limitations of inadequate resources—particularly in the face of the movement towards the increasing globalization of markets.

Partly in response to these forces, there has been a dramatic growth of strategic alliances between companies over the last decade, particularly in technology and marketing. As an OECD report commented in 1986:

> The spectacular growth of international interfirm technical co-operation agreements represents one of the most important and novel developments in the first half of the 80's.

Porter and Fuller (1986) focus on the basic purpose of an alliance when they say:

> Coalitions arise when performing a value chain activity with a partner is superior to any other way. ... Coalitions can be a valuable tool in many aspects of global strategy, and the ability to exploit them will be an important source of international advantage.

However, many commentators were still suspicious of alliances as a second-best solution that, disturbingly, was likely to break up under pressure. A more complete theoretical understanding of the basis for the development of strategic alliances, however, is needed before these fears can be allayed, and alliances are accepted as being just as stable and as viable as any other organizational form for conducting competitive business.

It is clearly not logical to claim that, in some undefined way, the 'best' solution to producing and selling products is either to operate in a perfectly competitive market or through an integrated company. The factors that determine an organization's viability depend not on whether it represents a market or an integrated company, but on the nature and volatility of the internal and external environment and, equally important, on the behaviour of the executive decision makers. Thus, success, or indeed failure, can come to a variety of forms—integrated companies, fragmented markets—and to a variety of types of co-operating enterprises.

The most common motivations behind the formation of strategic alliances are generally well known, as Aiken and Hage (1968) summarize succinctly in a sentence: 'Organisations go into joint ventures because of the need for resources, notably money, skill and manpower.'

More analytically, Pfeffer and Nowak (1976) and later Porter and Fuller (1986) suggest similar reasons for concluding strategic alliances:

1.   To achieve, with one's partner, economies of scale and of learning.
2.   To gain access to the benefits of the other firm's assets, be they technology, market access, capital, production capacity, products, or workforce.
3.   To reduce risk by sharing it, notably in terms of capital requirements, but also often R&D.
4.   To help shape the market, e.g. to withdraw capacity in a mature market.

Another motive behind the conclusion of strategic alliances is the need for speed in reaching the market (Lei and Slocum, 1991). In the current economic world, first-mover advantages are becoming of paramount importance, and often the conclusion of an alliance between a technologically strong company with new products and a company with strong market access is the only way to take advantage of an opportunity.

There may also be opportunities through the medium of alliances for the achievement of synergies that extend beyond the mere pooling of assets and include such matters as process rationalization and/or systems improvement.

CO-OPERATIVE STRATEGIES

A co-operative strategy adopted by a company may become at least as important as a competitive strategy in achieving competitive advantage. A useful way of categorizing such co-operative relationships might be to consider a spectrum running in ascending levels of integration from markets to hierarchies, with the market end of the spectrum dominated by the price mechanism and the hierarchy end by organizational fiat. Between the extremes of markets and hierarchies, there is a range of inter-organizational forms of ascending levels of integration, which may be assumed to exist because the partners find that the integration works well. As Barnard (1968) puts it: 'The efficiency of a co-operative system is its capacity to maintain itself by the individual satisfactions it affords.' Arm's-length market relationships at the base of the triangle frequently develop into established suppliers and distributors, and may then develop further into co-operative networks, as illustrated in Figure 1.2.

In a network, each member has access to specialized skills and competencies to meet special situations without the need to meet the overheads involved in developing the competencies internally. As Powell (1990) notes: 'The basic assumption of network relationships is that one party is dependent on resources controlled by another, and that there are gains to be had by pooling resources.' But, on the other hand, he states that 'all the parties to network forms of exchange have lost some of their ability to dictate their own future and are increasingly dependent on the activities of others'.

Further up the ladder of integration come the closely knit subcontractor networks, such as the Japanese *keiretsu*, or, nearer home, Marks and Spencer's close relationships with its suppliers, in which annual prices are fairly determined to give the supplier an acceptable margin, product is scheduled over a long period and delivered as required, and the purchasing firm puts very demanding inspectors into the

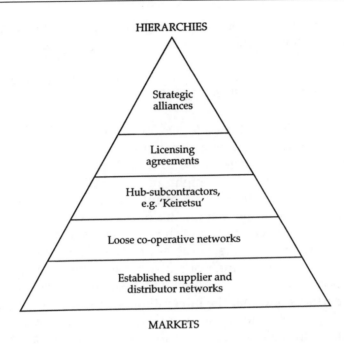

HIERARCHIES

Strategic
alliances

Licensing
agreements

Hub-subcontractors,
e.g. 'Keiretsu'

Loose co-operative networks

Established supplier and
distributor networks

MARKETS

Figure 1.2   The intermediate organizational forms between markets and hierarchies

supplying firm to ensure product quality. The next level comprises licensing agreements, in which the relationship between the licensor and the licensee is integrated from the viewpoint of activities in a defined area, but both retain their separate identities and ownership. Between licensing agreements and complete hierarchies, where rule by price (markets) is replaced by rule by fiat (hierarchies) come strategic alliances.

It is often assumed that the particular organizational form will be chosen that fits the specific circumstances of the relationship between the set of activities and the environment, and that the pressures of natural selection will cause inappropriate organizational forms to fail. However, such organizational failure may not be so automatic, and many inappropriate organizational forms continue even if they creak a little, because the strong sources of competitive advantage that the firm possesses enable acceptable financial performance to be achieved, and allay any calls for major reorganization.

Strategic alliances may be defined as:

A particular mode of inter-organisational relationship in which the partners make substantial investments in developing a long-term collaborative effort, and common orientation. (Mattsson, 1988)

This definition excludes inter-companies projects that have a beginning and preordained end, and loose co-operative arrangements without long-term commitment. In establishing the 'collaborative effort and common orientation' the alliance partners forsake a competitive strategy in relation to each other in agreed areas of activity, and embark on a strategy of co-operation.

Throughout the 1980s and into the 1990s not only alliances but overall co-operative forms of doing business have grown rapidly, and continue to increase as firms of all sizes and nationalities, in an increasing number of industries and countries perceive value in them. Collective or co-operative strategies and competitive strategies may now be thought of as being in a position of equal importance, as Bresser and Harl (1986) commented:

Whether competitive or collective strategies prevail at any one point in time appears largely irrelevant for obtaining viability and long-term stability. What is relevant is the ability to react to instabilities by switching from more collective forms of strategising to more competitive ones and vice-versa.

Strategic alliances, joint ventures, dynamic networks, constellations, co-operative agreements and collective strategies all make an appearance and develop significance.

In harmony with the growth of co-operative managerial forms, the reputation of co-operation seems to be enjoying a notable revival, to set against the hitherto dominant strength of the competitive model as a model of resource allocation efficiency. The term 'strategic alliances' has only recently achieved common usage to describe collaborations between firms. Until the mid-1980s the term 'joint ventures' was much more common, and covered a wide range of forms of inter-firm collaboration.

The obvious problem with co-operating with your competitor is the possible appropriation of your secrets. If this is the case, then what is the cause of this revival of the popularity of alliances, and how can co-operation be justified? A look at the situation found in the Prisoner's Dilemma situation described below shows how co-operation can be the best policy for both partners.

In 1951 Merrill Flood of the Rand Corporation developed a model that was later termed the Prisoner's Dilemma by Albert Tucker. It addresses the issue of how, individually, we balance our innate inclination to act selfishly, against the collective rationality of individual sacrifice for the sake of the common good. John Casti (1991) in his book *Paradigms Lost* illustrates the difficulty effectively:

> In Puccini's opera Tosca, Tosca's lover has been condemned to death, and the police chief Scarpia offers Tosca a deal. If Tosca will bestow her sexual favours on him, Scarpia will spare her lover's life by instructing the firing squad to load their rifles with blanks. Here both Tosca and Scarpia face the choice of either keeping their part of the bargain or double-crossing the other. Acting on the basis of what is best for them as individuals both Tosca and Scarpia try a double-cross. Tosca stabs Scarpia as he is about to embrace her, while it turns out that Scarpia has not given the order to the firing squad to use blanks. The dilemma is that this outcome, undesirable for both parties, could have been avoided if they had trusted each other and acted not as selfish individuals, but rather in their mutual interest.

Analytically there are two parties and both have the options of co-operating (C) or defecting (D). As shown in the 2 × 2 matrix (Figure 1.3). If each has a maximum value of 3 (a positive benefit with no compromise involved) and a minimum value of 0, then the possible outcomes and values for A are:

		Co-operate	Defect
Row player	Co-operate	R = 3, R = 3 Reward for mutual co-operation	S = 0, T = 5 Sucker's payoff and temptation to defect
	Defect	T = 5, S = 0 Temptation to defect and sucker's payoff	P = 1, P = 1 Punishment for mutual defection

NOTE   The payoffs to the row chooser are listed first

Figure 1.3   The prisoner's dilemma

- *A defects and B co-operates: A scores 3 (and B scores 0: Total 3).* Tosca gets all she wants without making any sacrifices. This would have happened if Tosca had killed Scarpia, and Scarpia had loaded the rifles with blanks, thus enabling Tosca's lover to escape.
- *A co-operates and B co-operates: A scores 2 (and B scores 2: Total 4).* Tosca, although saving her lover's life, has to submit sexually to Scarpia in order to do so, which it is presumed represents a sacrifice for her. Similarly, Scarpia's compromise involves not killing Tosca's lover.
- *A defects and B defects: A scores 1 (and B scores 1: Total 2).* This is what happened. At least Tosca has killed the evil Scarpia, but he in turn has killed her lover. Not a successful outcome for Tosca or Scarpia, however, but marginally better for her than the fourth possibility.
- *A co-operates and B defects: A scores 0 (and B scores 3: Total 3).* This is the worst outcome from Tosca's viewpoint. She has surrendered herself to Scarpia, but he has still executed her lover. This is the 'sucker's payoff', and to be avoided if possible at all costs.

The dilemma is that, since Tosca (A) does not know what Scarpia (B) will do, then rationally she is likely to defect in order to avoid the 'sucker's payoff'. Thus she may score 3 if Scarpia is as good as his word and she can make him the sucker. She will at least score 1. However, if both co-operate they will each score 2, which is the best joint score available. Yet in the absence of trust it is unlikely to be achieved.

Thus, in the situation of a strategic alliance, the optimal joint score can only be achieved through genuine trusting co-operation; yet this may be difficult to achieve if both parties in the alliance are overly concerned not to be the sucker, and are reluctant to release their commercial secrets, in case their partner decides to defect with them. This was the problem that Robert Axelrod (1984) set out to address in an interesting set of experiments. The issues he addressed were:

1. How can co-operation get started in a world of egoists?
2. Can individuals employing co-operative strategies survive better than their unco-operative rivals?
3. Which co-operative strategies will do best?

Axelrod invited a number of academics to participate in a contest pitting different strategies against one another in a computer tournament. Each participant was to supply the proposed best strategy for playing a sequence of Prisoner's Dilemma interactions in a round-robin tournament. The winning strategy was the simplest, namely Anatol Rapoport's strategy of Tit-for-tat. It had only two rules:

1. Co-operate on the first encounter.
2. Thereafter do what your opponent did on the previous round.

Such a strategy was a forgiving one, which implied a willingness to initiate and reciprocate co-operation. If both partners did indeed co-operate on the first round, then co-operation would continue; however, if only one co-operated on the first round and the other defected (thus creating a sucker) in the first round, then the co-operator would defect in the second round to show the defector the error of its ways and the penalty for defection. The results were confirmed in a second tournament. The conclusions were: (a) be co-operative and forgiving, and (b) retaliate when appropriate, without being vindictive. Axelrod summed up:

> Tit-for tat won the tournaments not by beating the other player but by eliciting behaviour from the other player that allowed both to do well. . . . So in a non-zero sum world, you do not have to do better than the other player to do well for yourself. This is especially true when you are interacting with many different players. . . . The other's success is virtually a prerequisite for doing well yourself.'

Applied to strategic alliances, this series of experiments suggests a number of things:

1. The rational strategy of defection (competition) applies on the assumption of a zero-sum game, and a non-repeatable experience—i.e. if you are only in business for a single trade (e.g. buying a souvenir in a bazaar in Morocco), defection is a rational strategy for you.

2. As soon as the game becomes a non-zero-sum, e.g. through scale economies, and/or it is known that the game will be played over an extended period of time, the strategy of defection is likely to become suboptimal, i.e. to co-operate and keep your bargain is a better strategy for both players. At the very least if you do not co-operate it will harm your reputation and you will be known as someone who cannot be trusted.

3. In these circumstances, forgiving co-operative strategies are likely to prove the most effective.

Thus, for example, a partner who defects (steals secrets) in an alliance will find his or her gains short-lived as the alliance founders, and the existence of available future partners will become somewhat limited as he or she will be preceded by a reputation for defection. A good co-operator, however, will develop the opposite reputation, and will experience attractive partnership propositions.

MOTIVES FOR ALLIANCES

Globalization of markets and technologies is currently probably the strongest force leading to the development of alliances. The most popular modern technologies—i.e. micro-electronics, genetic engineering and advanced material sciences—are all subject to truly global competition. Stopford and Turner (1985) suggest the following major forces leading to globalization:

(a) technology, principally through the micro-electronics revolution
(b) cultural evolution, i.e. the homogenization of tastes through media and other forces
(c) the breaking down of barriers (e.g. deregulation) and economic integration.

Thus global technologies make the world a smaller place through improved communication and facilitate the design and manufacture of products with truly global appeal.

Failure to appreciate this in the USA may well have been a major factor leading to the growing predominance of Japan in international markets. US companies co-operate with Japanese companies, and export their technological expertise. The Japanese carry out the production function, while the US firms accept functional substitution, instead of engaging in organizational learning. The Japanese then improve the technology, quality and costs, and successfully attack the US market.

Technology has also been a key factor behind the dramatic growth of co-operative agreements in the 1980s. Osborn and Baughn's research (1987) showed that 189 co-operative agreements were registered in Japanese and US companies between October 1984 and October 1986. Of these, 20 per cent involved co-operative R&D and 50 per cent crossed industrial boundaries but still had a strong technological content. An international alliance may be an effective way of spreading technology.

THE FEDERATED ENTERPRISE

Organizational form has also been dramatically influenced by the globalization of markets and technologies, through a decline in the automatic choice of the integrated multinational corporation as the only instrument appropriate for international business development. The movement away from the traditional concept of the firm is accentuated by the growth of 'Federated Organizations', as Professor Handy describes them (1992), of which perhaps the largest recent example is IBM, one of the most powerful multinational corporations in the world. IBM decided in 1991, after experiencing a significant decline in performance and suspecting a loss of competitive advantage, to make a radical restructure of its operations from that of an integrated worldwide firm with a strong single culture, to that of a federation of 14 potentially competitive companies. The culture shock has been so great, and the immediate results so mixed, that the chief executive resigned and his successor has come from outside the computer industry. The IBM of the

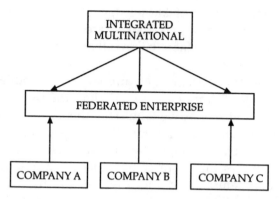

Figure 1.4   Federated enterprises developing from both directions

future is likely to be a federated enterprise, although it is evident that the company has not yet adapted successfully to such a radically changed paradigm.

The recent growth of alliances approaches the flexible transnational structure from the other end, i.e. the amalgamation of previously independent resources and competencies in contrast to the unbundling into a federal structure of previously hierarchically controlled resources and competencies (see Figure 1.4).

THE RESOURCE-BASED THEORY OF COMPETITIVE ADVANTAGE

The search for sustainable competitive advantage is of course an ongoing activity of every organization, yet this is a factor that cannot be measured directly. Its extent can only be inferred from the measurement of other factors such as profit, market share and sales turnover. It is nonetheless the Holy Grail that all firms seek to find and to maintain. Coyne (1986) identifies it as stemming from:

1.   Customers' perception of a consistent superiority of the attributes of one firm's products over its competitors.
2.   This being due to a capability gap.
3.   The capability gap being durable over time.
4.   The superiority being difficult to imitate.

It is this configuration of knowledge, skills, core competencies and superior products that strategic alliances seek to achieve, where the partners believe that they cannot achieve it alone.

Strategic alliances occur in a variety of forms, but are most frequently, at least implicitly, founded on the resource based theory of competitive advantage. This theory, as expounded by Professor Grant (1991), holds that competitive advantage is most productively sought by an examination of a firm's existing resources and core competencies, an assessment of their profit potential, and the selection of strategies based upon the possibilities this reveals. As Snyder and Ebeling (1993) put it:

> . . . the firm is a system of activities, not a portfolio of individual products or services. Some activities are performed so much better than the competition and are so critical to end products or services that they can be described as core competencies. When a series of activities are organized into a system that works better than the sum of its parts, this business process can also create competitive advantage, even if component activities by themselves do not.

The task is then to assess the current core competencies the firm possesses, and, in relation to the perceived potential profit opportunities, fill whatever resource or competency gap is revealed after taking an inventory of existing resources and competencies. This is where strategic alliances are most beneficial. They are 'a way of extending resources and capabilities, hence core competencies in order to develop sustainable competitive advantage' (Grant, 1991).

Figure 1.5 suggests how the make/buy/ally decision should be influenced by the strategic importance of the activity in question and by the firm's competence at carrying it out. Under this schema alliances should be formed if the activity is at least moderately strategically important and the firm is not too adept at carrying it out.

Insight into strategy options can only be perceived, of course, by an examination of the external environment and the internal strengths of the firm. However, the emphasis

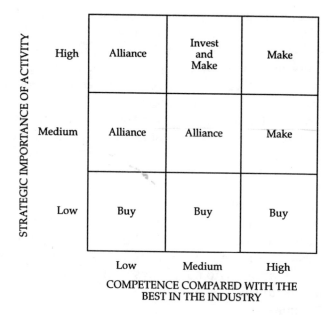

Figure 1.5   The make/buy/alliance matrix

placed upon the sequence in which this exercise is carried out is of some importance. Throughout the 1980s, strongly influenced by Porter's *Competitive Strategy* (Porter, 1980), the strategic process has been most commonly described as follows:

1. Analyse the industrial environment for opportunities.
2. Assess the internal capacity available to take advantage of these opportunities.
3. Identify, evaluate and select the appropriate strategies.
4. Implement the chosen strategy.

The concept behind this process is that the attractiveness of the industry is the prime determinant of profitability. However, as can be seen from PIMS data (Buzzell and Gale, 1987), the variation of profit levels in firms *within* industries is at least as great as that *between* industries. Furthermore, the undoubted profit record of the Hanson Group and others—who have a fundamental strategy that frequently involves investing in apparently unattractive industries but runs companies efficiently—casts further doubt on this emphasis. It can also lead a firm, that believes it has identified an attractive opportunity, to embark on an investment in that opportunity area without paying sufficient attention to the question of whether the supposed opportunity actually builds upon its existing core competencies.

The resource-based theory of competitive advantage suggests that a firm should not invest in an enterprise that is not strongly related to its own core competencies. The theory holds that only strategies based upon existing core competencies could lead to the acquisition and maintenance of sustainable competitive advantage. Snow and Hrebiniak (1980) found that firms concentrating on a distinctive competence, consistent with their chosen strategy, regularly outperformed competitors. The resource-based approach emphasizes that firms do not always tend towards similarity, and markets towards commodity status, in a situation of stable equilibrium.

> The exclusive focus on equilibrium and structural dimensions is absent. Instead disequilibrium and process dynamics are primary. (Amit and Schoemaker, 1993)

If the opportunity requires certain competencies in addition to those already present within the firm, a strategic alliance with a partner with complementary skills and resources may represent a low-risk method of overcoming that deficiency.

THE RESOURCE DEPENDENCY PERSPECTIVE

A strong motivation for setting up alliances can be found in a further theory with a similar sounding name, the Resource Dependency Perspective. This theory, developed by Professors Pfeffer and Salancik in 1978, proposes that the key to organizational survival is the ability to acquire and maintain resources. Thus, in the last resort it is not merely organizational efficiency, but organizational power and the capacity of the organization to preserve itself that determines competitive survival. The unit of analysis for the Resource

Dependency Perspective (RDP) is the organization : environment relationship, not the individual transaction. As Pfeffer
and Salancik (1978) have stated: 'Problems arise not merely
because organizations are dependent on their environment,
but because the environment is not dependable.'

To deal with this uncertainty, firms attempt to manage
their environment by co-operating with key parts of it—for
example, by forming alliances. An RDP approach treats the
environment as a source of scarce resources, and therefore
views the firm as dependent on other firms in the environment. The resource dependency theory stems from the much
earlier theory of social exchange, which holds that where
organizations have similar objectives, but various kinds or
different combinations of resources at their disposal, it will
often be mutually beneficial to the organizations in the
pursuit of their goals to exchange resources (Levine and
White, 1961; Litwak and Hylton, 1962). Classical international
trade theory is based on similar foundations of 'comparative
advantage'.

Thompson (1967) suggests that the rationale for organizations is to seek to reduce sources of uncertainty, and enter
into exchange relationships to achieve a negotiated and more
predictable environment. 'Sources of uncertainty' are scarcity
of resources and lack of knowledge of (a) how the environment will fluctuate, (b) the available exchange partners and
(c) the costs of transacting with them.

The degree of a firm's dependence is a function of the
critical nature of the resources in the exchange to the parties
involved, and of the number of and ease of access to
alternative sources of supply. Where there are few alterna-
tives, and the resources are essential, a state of dependency
exists. This creates a power differential between trading
partners, and the dependent firm faces the problem of how to
manage its resources with the resulting loss of independence,
since unchecked resource dependence leads to a state of
strategic vulnerability.

Such strategic vulnerability can be tackled in a number of
ways. For example, Western firms may attempt multiple
sourcing of materials and components, internal restructuring,
or merger and acquisition; Japanese firms may try to

establish their semi-captive suppliers within *keiretsu* groups. The establishment of a strategic alliance can thus be regarded as an attempt by a firm or firms to reduce strategic vulnerability, and hence to overcome perceived constraints on their autonomy in choosing their strategic direction. Strategic alliances can be seen as attempts by firms to establish a negotiated environment, and thus to reduce uncertainty. On the basis of this argument, most alliances will occur when the level of competitive uncertainty is greatest, since 'The level of competitive uncertainty is positively correlated with efforts to manage that uncertainty' (Pfeffer and Salancik, 1978).

In RDP-motivated alliances, both parties typically strive to form relationships with, where possible, similar-sized firms with whom balance can be achieved at minimum cost and with a desirable level of satisfaction and determinacy. This approach is echoed by Kotter (1979) in what he calls the external dependence perspective, thus:

> organizations cope (*inter alia*) with external dependence by establishing favourable relationships with those they are dependent upon and with alternative sources of support in their domain.

He goes on to state that one way of doing this is by means of: 'joint ventures and other complex coalitions with other organizations'.

THE LEARNING ORGANIZATION

Strategic alliances are probably most frequently formed from resource dependency motives. The ability of the partners to achieve and sustain competitive advantage in their chosen market is strongly influenced by the priority they devote to corporate learning on their alliance agenda, and they must seek to cause the alliance to evolve in a direction based on that learning. As Kogut (1988) stated:

> A joint venture is used for the transfer of organizationally

embedded knowledge that cannot be easily blueprinted or packaged through licensing or market transactions.

In a sense, corporate learning can be seen as the dynamic counterpart to the resource dependency theory of the organization. Thus a firm will diagnose its resource and skill deficiencies in relation to a particular external challenge, and through the process of deliberate and planned corporate learning will attempt to remedy its weaknesses.

Alliances that are genuinely strategic should be competence driven, explicitly adding to the task or knowledge system or to the organizational memory of each partner. The idea of the organization as a residuary for learning is widely acclaimed. Decision theory emphasizes the importance of the search for information to enable organizations to make informed choices. Hamel (1991) stresses the role of learning as a source of competitive advantage through the development of unique competencies, and Senge (1992) describes learning organizations as the only survivors of the future.

Corporate learning may be regarded as having two fundamental dimensions:

1. Individual learning
2. Organizational learning

Individual learning may be rational (how to work a computer) or intuitional (learned unconsciously, like riding a bicycle). However it is achieved, individual learning adds to the competencies of the organization, but is in theory easily appropriated, as the individual with the developed competence may be attracted to another firm.

Organizational learning develops at a level beyond that of the individual, and becomes embedded in the rituals, routines and systems of a firm—in its culture. As such, it is more deeply rooted in its core competencies, and may therefore survive the tenure of individuals. Corporate organizational learning may be construed as consisting of both types described above.

Even faced with success stories of the evolution of an alliance through mutual learning leading to competitive advantage, nagging doubts may well remain about the role of value appropriation in the form of learning by the partners, and of the consequent stability of the alliance. It is often suggested in fact that the alliance is an inherently unstable and transitory arrangement, and, undoubtedly, given opportunistic attitudes by the partners, it can be.

'Learning' and 'stability' are two terms that need to be 'unpacked' if they are to be used productively in argument. Perhaps owing to the influence of the concept of 'equilibrium' from the economists, stability is felt to be a state after which all wise organizations hanker. It is a 'good' thing, but what do we mean by 'stability' in a world that is constantly changing? In an interview in 1992, Professor Teramoto of Japan commented:

> It is often said that alliances are unstable. This is based on a failure to understand business life. Stability is in instability, and instability in stability. All are based on change, and this is the norm. Alliances are therefore no more unstable or stable than any other organizational form. All react by changing as they adapt to a constantly changing environment.

The often cited comparison of an alliance with a marriage is pertinent here. Marriages could be regarded as unstable as they currently have a high failure rate. In fact they have many of the qualities of strategic alliances. The partners retain separate identities but collaborate over a whole range of activities. Stability is threatened if one partner becomes excessively dependent on the other, or if one partner is perceived to be receiving all the benefits. None the less, successful marriages are stable, and for the same reason as successful alliances. They both depend on trust, commitment, mutual learning, flexibility and a feeling by the partners that they are stronger together than apart. Many businesses point to the need to negotiate decisions in alliances as a weakness, in contrast to companies, where hierarchies make decisions. This is to confuse stability with clarity of decision making, and would lead to the suggestion that dictatorships are more stable than democracies.

In this analogy, it is commitment to the belief that the

alliance represents the best available arrangement that is the foundation of its stability. The need for resolution of the inevitable tensions in such an arrangement can as easily be presented as a strength than as an inherent problem. It leads to the need to see, debate and evaluate contrasting viewpoints.

How then is the learning issue resolved, and does it influence alliance evolution? In terms of the possibilities presented by an alliance, there are a number of different types of learning each with different implications. Technological learning is a mixture of the technology describable in blueprints plus the know-how involved in their use. Process learning is more deeply embedded in the culture of the partner, and is therefore more difficult to transplant. Opportunity learning involves practical matters, such as: Who are the best suppliers? What is the best way of obtaining skilled labour? Who are the best agents? Finally, a learning philosophy is an attitude that is very difficult to define but is probably the most crucial key to ultimate alliance success; it is almost guaranteed to transform the whole nature and culture of the company.

The ease with which learning takes place within an alliance depends, first, on the type of learning and, second, on the relationship between the nature of the learning and the condition of the would-be learner.

SUMMARY

Many collaborative activities between companies are arranged for short-term gains in order to deal with temporary situations. These obscure the nature of the true strategic alliance, in which the intent is a learning one, in the cause of joint sustainable competitive advantage, and the extension of individual and joint core competencies.

The above propositions suggest a number of key factors:

- The key to continued success is not skill (or product) substitution, but the ability and determination to learn from one's partners the competencies in which one is deficient.

- Sensitivity to cultural differences is vital to this process, but this is a different thing from the requirement for cultural similarity when selecting a partner. This latter characteristic may not be an advantage, since dissimilarities provide learning opportunities.

- To achieve genuine learning, 'transparency' is necessary, i.e. a willingness of the partners to transfer knowledge is necessary, and this can only be brought about through positive inter-partner attitudes. In this regard commitment, trust and flexibility are the attitudes most necessary for success in an alliance. If some personal bonding can be achieved between the partners, this also aids successful alliance development.

- Finally, it is obviously important to choose a partner with complementary assets and abilities, but after that point the alliance will only succeed through the mutually supportive behaviour of the partners, and a willingness by both to teach each other those areas that require development.

The next chapter analyses the variety of alliance forms, and suggests some principles to guide partner selection.

2 Alliance variety and partner selection

There is a wide variety of different forms of alliance: for example, technology development coalitions, marketing and distribution agreements, operations and logistics coalitions, single country and multi-country alliances, joint ventures creating a daughter company from two or more parent partners, minority share exchange agreements, and licensing agreements. This list is by no means exhaustive and omits co-operative arrangements that are more flexible and more in the nature of networks.

Writers on the subject of strategic alliances are by no means united in their methods of classification. Ghemawat *et al.* (1986) classify all alliances as either x, i.e. vertical coalitions (alliances between partners carrying out different activities in the value chain) or y, i.e. horizontal coalitions (partners carrying out the same activity in the value chain). They also classify them by their legal nature (41 per cent joint ventures, 16 per cent licences, 12 per cent supply agreements in their sample) and according to their functional areas of concern (20 per cent technological including exploration, 42 per cent operations and logistics, 22 per cent marketing sales and service).

Classification of strategic alliances are made in so many different ways that it is difficult to decide which form is the most useful for analytical purposes. Garrette and Dussauge (1990) use the terms *horizontal* strategic alliances, linking competing firms operating in the same industry, and *vertical* strategic alliances, linking buyers and suppliers in separate industries, but capable of being integrated into the same business system. They consider these two types of alliance as quite distinct in nature. The horizontal alliance, by linking competitors, blurs the distinction between rivalry and co-operation at least within a defined domain. Vertical alliances, however, between manufacturer and supplier remove much of the uncertainty of price and availability from the relationship, at the cost of potentially sacrificing the efficiency regulating power of the price mechanism. In addition, there is a third variety, described by Bronder and Pritzl (1992) as 'diagonal alliances', which apply to co-operative activities between companies in different industries, and there are of course many hybrid forms.

Professor Pucik (1988) suggests that, in the past, alliances were mainly concerned with reducing capital investment needs and lowering the risk of entry to new markets, but that the current emphasis is mainly concerned with taking advantage of the increased speed of technological change, and adjusting to the rapidly growing competitiveness of global markets. The types of alliance in Pucik's classifications are:

1.   Alliances for technological change, e.g. cross-licensing
2.   Co-production and OEM agreements
3.   Sales and distribution ties
4.   Joint product development programmes
5.   The creation of joint ventures.

All have the aim, he states, of '. . . attaining the position of global market leadership through internalisation of key added value competencies'.

Professor Kanter (1989) takes a similar view in more down to earth language: 'Getting the benefits of what another organisation offers without the risks and responsibility of owning it, is the ultimate form of leverage.' She identifies three fundamental types of alliance:

1.   Multi-company service consortia, e.g. for R&D
2.   Opportunistic alliances set up to take advantage of specific situations, e.g. most joint ventures
3.   Stakeholder alliances, referred to by other researchers as vertical alliances, or alliances between companies at

different parts of the value chain, e.g. supply/producer complementary coalitions.

Consortia, she notes, try to achieve the benefit of large-scale activity by pooling resources, e.g. MCC was set up to compete with the Japanese in R&D. In areas of new technology, these alliances are very popular between companies that are normally competitors. However, they often founder, she states, as a result of a low level of commitment by each member, and from having mediocre seconded staff. Opportunistic joint ventures, in which each partner supplies the competencies that the other lacks, are, she believes, the most unstable of alliance forms. The principal driving forces are technological transfer and market access. However, owing to their opportunistic nature, these alliances find difficulty in achieving the necessary robustness when circumstances change, especially if they change asymmetrically for the parties. Stakeholder alliances institutionalize previous interdependence, and are often quality or innovation driven, i.e. a firm treats a supplier as a partner in order to increase quality. These alliances should be stable, as they have a high commitment and little competition.

There is, therefore, little unanimity among writers when classifying the various types of strategic alliance. Most of the classification systems listed above do not meet the criteria of being composed of mutually exclusive categories; nor are they usefully descriptive of the essential nature of the alliance or of a specific organizational form in which generalizable research could be carried out.

ALLIANCE TYPES

A form of classification can be adopted if the alliances are classified along three axes, namely:

1. The scope of the alliance: i.e. focused or complex
2. The creation or otherwise of a new corporate legal entity, i.e. a joint venture or a more flexible collaboration

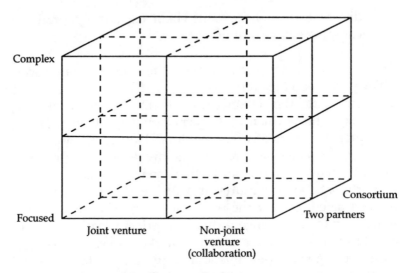

Figure 2.1   The strategic alliance options

3.   The number of alliance partners, i.e. two partners or a consortium.

Thus the types can be represented, as in Figure 2.1, with focused/complex, joint venture/collaboration and two partners/consortium as the three axes.

Focused alliance

The focused alliance is a collaborative arrangement between two or more companies, set up to meet a clearly defined set of circumstances in a particular way. Thus, for example, a US company seeking to enter the European market with a given set of products, may form a focused alliance with a European distribution company as its means of entry. The US company will provide the product and the market and sales literature, while the European company provides the salesforce and local know-how. The precise form of arrangement may vary, but the nature of the alliance is focused, with clear remits and understanding of respective contributions and rewards. Thus, in November 1989 Cincinnati Bell Information Systems set up an alliance with Kingston Communications of Hull,

England, to market CBIS's automated telecommunications equipment throughout the European Community. CBIS provided the equipment and Kingston provided the sales effort.

Complex alliance

The complex alliance may involve certain parts of or even the entire organization of each partner. The companies recognize that, in combination, they form a potentially much more powerful competitive enterprise than they do individually, and while they are willing to co-operate with each other over a wide range of activities, they nevertheless wish to retain their separate identities and overall aspirations. Rover/ Honda is a good example of a complex alliance. Currently it includes joint R&D, joint manufacturing, joint development and sourcing of parts. The companies remain separate, however, in the critical marketing and sales areas, and both companies retain clearly distinct images. The alliance involved a 20 per cent share exchange between Rover and the Honda UK manufacturing company, but this is not a necessary condition for this type of alliance. Indeed, since the sale of Rover to BMW the equity exchange is in the process of being cancelled.

Joint venture

A joint venture involves the creation of a legally separate company of which the alliance partners are normally founding shareholders. Thus, a US company may set up a joint venture with a UK company to market in the European Union. The partners normally provide finance and other support resources, including some personnel, until the venture is able to develop its own. The aim of the joint venture is typically that the new company should ultimately become a self-standing entity with its own aims, employees and resources. Unilever is a good example of a successful joint venture; it was set up in the 1920s by Dutch and British companies and is now a major multinational enterprise.

Collaboration

A collaboration is an alliance form that has no joint venture company to give it boundaries. It is therefore the most flexible, and potentially the least committed form of alliance—at least at the outset. Companies can form a collaboration on a very minimal basis to see how the enterprise develops, and allow it to deepen and broaden by introducing new projects over a period of time. As the collaboration requires no major initial commitment, it also has no limitations. It is probably the most appropriate form of co-operation when the extent of the possible relationship is impossible to foresee at the outset, when the alliance is not bounded by a specific business or set of assets, and when joint external commitment at a certain level is not specifically sought. The collaborative form may be most appropriate if the activity concerned is a core activity of the partners; if it is non-core, a joint venture may be more appropriate. Such guidelines, however, are often not crucial when choosing the form of alliance. The alliance of the Royal Bank of Scotland and Banco Santander is a good example of a successful collaboration. The banks collaborate over a wide range of activities, but have no single joint venture company to provide boundaries to the relationship.

Consortium

The consortium is a distinct form of strategic alliance. It has a number of partners, is normally a large-scale activity set up for a very specific purpose, and is managed in a hands-off manner by the contributing shareholders. Consortia are particularly common for large-scale projects in the defence industry, where massive funds and a wide range of specialist skills are required for success. Airbus Industrie is a consortium in which a number of European shareholders have set up an aircraft manufacturing company to compete in world markets with Boeing and McDonnell Douglas. Although the European shareholders were quite large themselves, they considered it was necessary to create a pool of funds and skills to ensure that they had sufficient resources for aircraft development, and chose to form an international consortium to achieve this. There are, then, eight possible combinations of strategic alliance, as illustrated in Figure 2.1.

1. Focused joint venture
    (focused/joint venture/two partners—FJV2)
2. Focused consortium
    (focused/joint venture/consortium—FJV>2)
3. Focused collaboration
    (focused/non-joint venture/two partners—FNJV2)
4. Focused multi-partner collaboration
    (focused/non- joint venture/consortium—FNJV>2)
5. Complex joint venture
    (complex/joint venture/two partners—CJV2)
6. Complex consortium
    (complex/joint venture/consortium—CJV>2)
7. Complex collaboration
    (complex/non-joint venture/two partners—CNJV2)
8. Complex multi-partner collaboration
    (complex/non-joint venture/consortium—CNJV>2)

Within this system it is apparent that some alliance arrangements are simpler and less irretrievably committing than others. It also seems probable that some types will develop out of others. Thus the simplest type of all is the focused collaboration where two partners agree to work together on a defined project. Given successful interaction, this may develop into a complex form of alliance, as did Rover/ Honda, or it may lead to the creation of a joint venture.

Focused two-partner joint ventures are also a simple and very popular form, set up to meet a very specific set of circumstances. If successful, these focused joint ventures are likely to develop new projects and move into the complex category.

Two-partner alliances may recruit further partners and move into the consortium form, as did the Royal Bank of Scotland and Banco Santander with IBOS, their pan-European electronics payments system. It is also possible for the alliance to develop hybrid characteristics, as occurred in the alliance between the Royal Bank of Scotland and Banco Santander when they decided, jointly, to acquire a German merchant bank, thereby adding a focused joint venture to their complex collaborative alliance.

Intuitively less likely paths of evolution, perhaps, may be from complex to focused, from consortium to two partner, or from joint venture to non-joint venture.

TESTING THE SYSTEM

In order to discover whether the classification system was useful, it was tested on a number of alliances recorded in the press over the past few years and subsequently captured on a database. It was clear that the classification system could readily be applied. The results were recorded and of the 228 alliances considered, the percentage breakdown of the configurations was as shown in Table 2.1. The cells of the cube can be analysed graphically as shown in Figure 2.2.

Thus, the establishment of joint venture companies to define the alliance boundaries was carried out in 69.5 per cent of the sample of alliances. This is intuitively sensible, since the creation of such a new entity can help to overcome many of the cultural, and ambiguous boundary issues that tend to make alliances so difficult to manage. The alliance was given a clearly defined focus in 67.5 per cent of the

Table 2.1   *Alliance classification*

Classification	%
1. Focused joint venture (FJV2)	31.0
2. Focused consortium (FJV>2)	20.0
3. Focused collaboration (FNJV2)	11.5
4. Focused multi-partner collaboration (FNJV>2)	5.0
5. Complex joint venture (CJV2)	14.5
6. Complex consortium (CJV>2)	4.0
7. Complex collaboration (CNJV2)	11.0
8. Complex multi-partner collaboration (CNJV>2)	3.0
Total	100.0

Two-partner

	MV	Coll.
Complex	14.5	11.0
Focused	31.0	11.5

Consortium

	JV	Coll.
Complex	4.0	3.0
Focused	20.0	5.0

Joint venture

	2 Part.	>2
Complex	14.5	4.0
Focused	31.0	20.0

Collaboration

	2 Part.	>2
Complex	4.0	3.0
Focused	20.0	5.0

Focused

	JV	Coll.
2 Partner	31.0	11.5
>2 Partner	20.0	5.0

Complex

	JV	Coll.
2 Partner	14.5	11.0
>2 Partner	4.0	3.0

Figure 2.2 Analysis of results in Table 2.1

sample cases. Lack of data on the alliance's history prevented a view being taken on how often a focused alliance evolved into a complex one. Consortia accounted for 32 per cent of the sample, and these were generally major examples of international collaboration between giant global corporations, often related to the defence and aerospace industries.

Perhaps unsurprisingly, the least popular alliance form was the complex multi-partner collaboration (CNJV>2). This could be regarded as virtually unmanageable, with its multiplicity of partners, complex agenda and lack of a joint venture company to concentrate attention. As such it has more of the characteristics of a network than of an alliance.

Some writers claim that it is not possible to assign particular alliance forms to particular sets of industrial or environmental circumstances in anything more than a very general way, and the adoption of a particular form may be more dependent on the personal preferences of the partners than on any objective factor. However, it seems probable that companies seeking a strategic alliance with a partner for the first time are likely to start with a focused joint venture or collaboration in order to discover more about their partner before attempting an involved relationship.

A few other general points can be made from an examination of the information contained in the data.

1. Major international projects involving massive capital and a wide variety of specialist skills seem to be generally carried out in consortium joint ventures (FJV>2 and CJV>2). Examples of this form abound; for instance, the consortium set up by Electricité de France with Powergen and National Power of the UK, and a number of German power company partners, to develop the electricity distribution system in the former East Germany; or the project commissioned by the Japanese government to develop a supersonic airplane was undertaken by an international consortium composed of Mitsubishi, Kawasaki and Ishikawayima-Harima of Japan, General Electric and Pratt and Whitney of the USA, Rolls-Royce of the UK and SNECMA of France.

2. Less commonly consortium alliances are set up in a purely collaborative form without a joint venture company (FNJV>2 or CNJV>2); for example, the consortium of Motoren und Turbinen Union of Munich, Rolls-Royce of the UK and Turbomeca of France to develop dual shaft modular design engines for the MTR390 of the Tiger anti-tank helicopter. In this case the work is to be shared between the partners—40 per cent Motoren und Turbinen, 40 per cent Turbomeca and 20 per cent Rolls-Royce—without the creation of a joint venture vehicle.

3. Despite the popularity of the joint venture for reasons outlined above, a substantial percentage of alliances operate without a separate company to define their relationship. Of

the sample, 22.5 per cent were alliances between two partners, and a further 8.0 per cent were multi-partner alliances, all without joint ventures. Indeed, the Rover/ Honda alliance operated very successfully for 14 years without a separate joint venture company to define, and also possibly to limit, its development.

Testing the system of classification on the data-base showed that three composite types of alliance accounted for 91.5 per cent of the sample. The two-partner joint venture was the most popular form (45 per cent), followed by the consortium joint venture (24 per cent) and the two-partner collaboration (22.5 per cent). Thus, three principal forms emerged from the analysis, i.e. the *joint venture*, the *consortium*, and the *collaboration*, and these are the basic forms that were subsequently used for the remainder of the investigation.

SELECTING A PARTNER

The choice of partner is clearly likely to be the main issue in the success of a joint enterprise, but it is an area very difficult to research by means of interviews or questionnaires, since the partners in an alliance feel duty bound to assert to an interviewer that they have chosen the right partner, even when, in their innermost thoughts, they have real doubts. The two basic qualities sought in a relationship with a partner are:

- strategic fit
- cultural fit.

This can be illustrated on the matrix shown in Figure 2.3. The optimal alliance partners will be in box (2), where they have both strategic and cultural complementarity. In contrast, partners in box (3) have little chance of being successful. They have no obvious way of achieving competitive advantage in the markets in which they operate, and their cultures are likely to clash. Partners in box (4) are unlikely to do much better, since, although they may be compatible, they still do not fit together strategically, and are therefore unlikely to be

	Low	High
High	(1) Alliance potential good given cultural adjustment	(2) OPTIMAL ALLIANCE SITUATION
Low	(3) No joint competitive advantage or compatibility	(4) Compatibility but no joint competitive advantage

STRATEGIC FIT

CULTURAL FIT

Figure 2.3　Matrix of cultural and strategic fit

effective in the market. There is more hope for partners in box (1), since they represent good strategic fit, and have the incentive to work on their cultural differences to reduce the potential conflict in this area. The strategic matrix can then give indications as to the selection of an appropriate partner. The question is: How can we identify accurately the factors that go to make up strategic fit and cultural fit?

Strategic fit

The fundamental issue in assessing strategic fit is whether their joint value chain seems likely to achieve sustainable competitive advantage for the partners, through the complementarity of their resource endowments and core competencies. If the answer is yes, then the problem of how to set up the alliance should not prove too intractable. If the combination of the partners' skills and resources seems unlikely to achieve competitive advantage, then irrespective of how the alliance is set up, it is unlikely to prove successful. The two significant aspects of the partners' capabilities are the *complementary nature of their skills and assets,* and the *potential*

synergies that can be seen. Both are necessary for success, but each is insufficient by itself. Two partners may have complementary assets—for example, one may have good products and the other a good salesforce—but unless these strengths are sufficiently synergistic to beat the competition, success cannot be guaranteed. Similarly, two management teams may display synergistic working methods, but without complementary assets the alliance is likely to have problems settling the issue of who does what, and how the joint organization is to function.

Given synergies between the companies and their complementary assets, the potential for achieving competitive advantage will be good, but this will not necessarily guarantee a successful and enduring alliance. For this to be likely, the balance of need between the partners must be similar in strength, although probably different in nature. It is probable that some form of resource dependency has brought the partners into alliance; however, one partner may only be mildly in need of the other's resources or skills, and be quite capable of buying them in the market if the partnership becomes difficult. The second partner, on the other hand, may need the first partner's resources desperately, and in this case partner 2 will become excessively dependent on partner 1, which will adversely affect the power balance within the alliance.

This may come about similarly if both partners are of a significantly different size. An alliance between a very large and a very small partner is unlikely to be successful in the long term, although, of course, it may lead to competitive advantage and to the more powerful partner buying the smaller partner on terms that are acceptable to both.

A further factor in strategic fit is that each partner must need some aspect of the other's resources. There is no strategic fit, for example, where one partner has good products but is resource dependent for marketing skills, and the other partner is cash rich but product deficient and also lacks marketing strength. In this set of circumstances one potential partner should probably seek a different partner that has strong marketing ability and values access to its products, or it should seek to strengthen its marketing by external recruitment. The other potential partner might consider an acquisition to make more effective use of its financial strength.

An important condition for continuing success in an alliance is that the long-term objectives of the partners should not conflict. This does not mean that they must necessarily have identical aims, which is unlikely in two or more companies determined to retain their separate identities. Thus, in an alliance one company may be concerned with developing its technology world wide, while the other wishes to economize on R&D expenditure by employing the partner's technology to develop its local market. There is no conflict in this; however, if both wish to develop globally, yet the one importing the technology has limited itself at the outset to being a local partner, future conflict will be difficult to avoid. The research showed that this was not an unknown problem in alliances, but suggested that it could be catered for through flexible attitudes.

Strategic fit, therefore, involves partners of similar size with similar strengths of mutual resource or skill requirement. They should have congruent objectives, and possess such complementary assets and potential mutual synergies as are likely to enable them to achieve competitive advantage through optimal use of their joint value chains.

Cultural fit

It is possible that an alliance will show tangible results justifying itself unconditionally on the grounds of meeting its declared objectives, but will still be in danger of foundering as a result of friction between the partners. This demonstrates the importance of cultural factors in the smooth running of an alliance. It is not important that the cultures of the partners be similar. If it were, few alliances would succeed, since cultural similarity between companies is extremely rare, especially between partners from different nationalities. Also, since organizational learning is a key to successful alliances, companies that are too similar are unlikely to have much to learn from each other. However, an attitude of understanding of cultural differences, and a willingness to compromise in the face of cultural problems, may well be vital to alliance effectiveness.

It is one thing to set up systems and devise organizations, but if mutual trust does not exist there is not likely to be a successful alliance. Trust is, however, difficult to insist upon, since it normally takes a long time to build and a short time to destroy. Alliances require it in their basic essence, and a philosophy that decrees 'I shall trust my partner until I have cause not to do so' is more likely to lead to success than one that says 'All partners are out for themselves; I will not trust mine until it has proved to be worthy of my trust'. The latter attitude frequently leads to the entry of an army of lawyers, and the sort of alliance documentation that may well destroy flexible potential at the outset.

Commitment is a similar factor to trust, in that it is vital to alliance effectiveness. It is difficult to pin down, but may be exemplified either positively or negatively in much of a partner's behaviour. It may, like trust, be shown at the top, and can be seen in the priority that is placed on alliance matters in board discussion, the quality of personnel allocated to alliance responsibilities, and the resources devoted to the alliance. It is equally important further down the organization, however, if the alliance is to work well on a day-to-day basis. An alliance without commitment and trust from the board downwards may soon wither away in its performance and importance to the partner companies.

Of course, if no more than a short-term relationship is expected, dealing with a transitory situation, and it is envisaged that the alliance will eventually be resolved by merger or dissolution, then the above characteristics are clearly less necessary, and a regime of mutual caution and detailed adherence to closely negotiated contractual arrangements may be the most appropriate policy. However, if the alliance is intended to be long term, the above cultural attitudes are likely to be vital ingredients in the alliance's success, namely a flexible attitude to cultural differences, an eagerness to learn from a partner that has different procedures, and strong commitment and mutual trust between the partners.

SUMMARY

This chapter has developed a system for classifying alliances, and has made a start at addressing the question of the type of alliance that may be most appropriate in certain circumstances. The classification system analyses alliances along three dimensions: their scope (focused or complex), their legal structure (separate joint venture company or a looser collaboration) and the number of members (two or a consortium). The chapter then discussed some criteria for choosing partners, concentrating on those that have strategic fit and those whose cultural sensitivities are such that they can reasonably be expected to develop a cultural fit.

3 The nature of alliances

MAKING DECISIONS IN A MAZE

When a decision has been made to seek a strategic alliance, no more has been achieved than a commitment to enter a very complex maze of further decision-making. The alliance-seeking company has to

(a) decide on the most appropriate criteria for partner selection;
(b) find and screen potential partners;
(c) identify the nature and strength of the partners' potential competitive advantage;
(d) assess their cultural compatibility;
(e) decide on the type of alliance to be set up, its nature and its boundaries, its capital (if any), its staffing and its targets and general objectives, its system of management and its longer-term objectives;
(f) determine the attitudes and business practices to be adopted between the partners.

Mistakes in addressing any of these complex issues may lead to failed alliances. If an organization is to emerge successfully from this maze of decision-making, it requires a clear map. This book attempts to provide some of the guidelines for the construction of such a map.

ALLIANCE DEVELOPMENT

If it is accepted that strategic alliances come about most frequently because the partners consider that their joint capabilities will enable them to gain a form of competitive advantage not available to them as separate entities, it is important to identify the conditions under which this situation is likely to arise.

There are a number of conditions that need to be satisfied if strategic alliances are to meet the above criteria. If these conditions obtain, then competitive advantage may be achieved through the medium of the alliance. Such advantage can only be achieved, as in non-alliance situations, through the creation of characteristics that are difficult to imitate yet are capable of generating profit. As Amit and Schoemaker suggest (1993), there are three basic sources of these mechanisms:

1.   Preferential market access, e.g. through brands
2.   Non-imitable cost advantages
3.   The possession of, or superior use of, specific assets or skills, particularly technology.

The stages of development of an alliance can be divided into three phases:

1.   Alliance formation
2.   Alliance management
3.   Alliance evolution.

Clearly stages 2 and 3 overlap in time, as stage 3 emerges from stage 2. For an alliance to demonstrate the primary characteristics of effectiveness, it needs to evolve from the initial pact, the process of evolution being strongly influenced by positive attitudes to corporate learning held by the partners.

Alliance formation

Alliances are formed for a wide variety of reasons. First, there is generally an external stimulus. In the 1980s and early

1990s, this has most commonly been the globalization or regionalization of markets. Companies that had been equipped quite adequately to prosper in national markets suddenly found themselves having to cope with major global competitors in their home market. A number of factors brought this about, including the 1992 EC single market directives, the dramatic improvement in worldwide communications, and the homogenization of tastes, and in many industries the same products were to be found in department stores in New York, Tokyo and London as Kenichi Ohmae (1989) points out.

Other external driving factors have been the ever-decreasing product life cycles and the development of global technologies. This has led to the need for larger investment commitments as firms had to engineer new products almost as soon as their latest products had been marketed. Few firms were adequately equipped to do this alone.

A further factor relating to technology was the growing need to have a sufficiently large volume of sales to be able to take advantage of economies of scale and scope that were available through modern automated manufacturing processes. It was essential to secure the low unit costs necessary to achieve competitive advantage. Additionally the world economy had, since the oil shocks of the 1970s, become an increasingly turbulent and uncertain place, and only corporations of large financial strength had the flexibility to cope with such uncertainty.

Most companies, even the largest, faced these external forces with concern, and strategic alliances became an important item on their agenda if they felt that they were deficient, in global terms, of resources, skills or what Prahalad and Hamel (1990) call 'core competencies'.

If they also felt the urgent need to place new products on the market to take advantage of major opportunities that might not remain long enough for their R&D to develop the products internally, and if they felt the need to economize with their finances and seek a partner to spread the risk, then they were strongly motivated towards seeking an alliance partner. Internally the theory of the Resource Dependency Perspective (RDP) frequently illustrates the underlying motive for the firm's realization of its need for allies, if it is to survive and prosper in the increasingly globalizing economy. As Astley (1984) put it: as environments become more turbulent and unpredictable, only co-operative activity can deal with them and 'the boundary between organizations and their environments begins to dissolve'.

The partner selected would, of course (as suggested above), need to possess complementary assets and capabilities, and have identifiable synergies; ideally the partner would have a compatible culture, and be a company with whom the firm believed it could achieve a sustainable competitive advantage that it could not achieve alone. In short, both partners would perceive their relationship as having a good strategic fit.

The selection of alliance form is probably also important, as different situations favour different forms. The collaboration form, for example, may be most appropriate for situations in which there is high uncertainty at the outset as to what tasks will be involved in the co-operative enterprise, and there is consequently a high need for flexibility between the partners. It may also be most appropriate where the partners do not immediately seek visible and specific initial commitments from each other, and where the alliance boundaries do not encompass specific assets or describe a clearly distinct business within each partner's portfolio.

As Gupta and Singh (1991) suggest, joint ventures are often formed where the alliance covers a distinct business area, generally not the core area of the companies, where the assets are distinct and separable from the partner companies, and where the partners feel the need to be committed to each other.

Consortia may be formed where the task is too large to be undertaken by only two companies from the level of financial commitment required to the variety of skills and competencies and, perhaps credibility with major clients, especially governments.

In the most successful alliances the partners' intentions at or even before formation will generally be to learn from their partner, and hence remove some of their individual competence deficiencies. This does not, however, necessarily mean that their intention is to absorb all their partner's know-how, and then subsequently establish themselves alone. This may happen in some alliances, as Beamish and Banks (1987) point out:

> The risk of leakage of proprietary knowledge . . . serves to limit the efficiency gains available through joint venture arrangements

—but not in the most enduring and successful ones.

Management of the alliance

A genuine strategic alliance is formed for the long term, as Roland Bertodo (1990) of The Rover Group underlines:

> Strategic alliances are not tools of convenience. They are . . . critical instruments in fulfilling corporate strategic objectives.

As such, the management system for running them needs to be established with as much care as that devoted to the choice of alliance form. Roehl and Truitt (1987) take the view that stormy open marriages are often the best in strategic alliances, but this seems to be a minority view. More common is the view that such relationships should ensure that the long-term goals of the partners should not be in conflict, although this does not mean that they need be identical. Levene and Byene (cited in Achrol *et al.*, 1990) point out, however:

> . . . over half the time top management spends on the average alliance goes into creating it, with involvement trailing off over time.

Important principles in this area involve agreeing good dispute resolution mechanisms, and, if possible, a divorce procedure to cater for the possibility that the alliance may cease to meet the needs of the parties as Professor Taucher of IMD suggests (1988). Perhaps the most important aspect is that attitudes need to be positive and flexible.

It is highly unlikely that the partners' structures or national cultures will be similar. If they are, of course, this may smooth the way for a harmonious working relationship. However, most strategic alliances are formed precisely because the partners are different, and are valued the more for their difference. The cultural atmosphere in the partner company is therefore unlikely to be similar. A sensitive attitude to cultural differences is therefore necessary if the alliance is to prosper, since the cultural differences in ways of operating are likely to lead to confusion in the partner companies. If attitudes are positive, sensitive and flexible, this need not have a negative impact on the alliance, and may lead to the partners absorbing what is best in each other's culture to their mutual benefit. Once more, learning from the partner is the key to effectiveness.

Two further attitudes are vital if the alliance is to be effective—namely, commitment and trust. Granovetter (1985) argues that interpersonal relationships are mechanisms to limit opportunism, and hence reduce the need for setting up a hierarchically run company. Commitment is demonstrated in the degree to which partners dedicate time and other resources to alliance matters, and are not discouraged by problems that arise. Killing (1988) stresses that the greater the degree of organizational and task complexity in an alliance, the greater the need for high commitment on the part of the managers to make it successful.

Trust is a more difficult area. Trust normally has to be earned in relationships, and this takes time. In alliances, however, it is suggested that an attitude that says 'I trust my partner, unless and until I have reason not to' is more likely to lead to positive results than the attitude which says 'I don't know my partner well. He or she will have to earn my trust over time'. In Hill's view, natural selection works here:

> In the long-run the invisible hand deletes actors who are habitually opportunistic as markets move towards a state of competitive equilibrium. (Hill, 1990)

A further important area is the establishment of systems to disseminate information throughout the company. In the absence of such systems there is a high risk that vital information, especially 'know-how', will remain with the partner and merely be used but not absorbed, or that it will go no further than the executives directly interfacing with their alliance partners and not become embedded in the partner companies' tacit knowledge fabric:

> International joint ventures point to the transferability of each partner's capability as a critical determinant of the allocation of benefits of the venture. (Grant, 1991)

Hamel (1991) also stresses the need for companies to appropriate the value they create, if they are to benefit from alliances in the future, and particularly if they are to maintain or increase their bargaining power in relation to their partner.

> Depending on its bargaining power a partner will gain a greater or lesser share of the fruits of the joint effort.

Thus we have the paradox that to gain from an alliance a partner needs to establish the ability to appropriate a substantial proportion of the value created by the alliance in the form of the successful internalization of new core competencies learned from the partner. However, the more successfully the firm can do this, the less it appears to need its partner and, hence, the bonds of the alliance become weaker.

Fortunately for the inherent value of alliances, like all good paradoxes, this is only an apparent contradiction and it arises from too static a view of an alliance. It assumes a finite set of competencies and skills, and that appropriation of value by one partner diminishes the pool available for the future. In fact it is likely that a successful alliance will, at the very least, produce value for the partner companies in the form of organizational learning, and also, at least in joint venture alliances, retain further value within the venture itself.

Alliance evolution

A key factor in the life of an alliance seems to be that, if it ceases to evolve, it starts to decay: 'Networks tend to disintegrate under the impact of entropy' (Thorelli, 1986).

Despite the continuance of the original agreement, management may start to lose interest in the liaison if nothing new comes from it. Bertodo of Rover is keenly aware of this, and is conscious of the need to maintain a balance between the two companies' relative need for each other. He sees it as trading 'packages' of competencies on a regular basis. There have so far been five basic 'trades' over the life of the Rover/ Honda alliance, all leading to continuous evolution. In an interview in 1991, Bertodo commented;

> As guardian of the company strategy . . . I have got to have something ready to trade if the company decides it needs to trade, which will depend on how fast it is learning. I think we don't learn fast enough, but I would say that wouldn't I?

The trading view, however, underlies a static 'fixed set of goods' philosophy. Yet the reality of a successful alliance is that it not only trades competencies but also realizes synergies. Whereas the Resource Dependency Perspective identifies a key part of a company's motivation for forming an alliance, the successful evolution of that alliance depends upon the realization of synergies between the companies, and the establishment of a durable competitive advantage for the partners that each could not realize alone. Evolution is about continuous value creation which will, in a successful collaboration alliance, be appropriated by the partners in a balanced fashion (see Figure 3.1). Some value will emerge in terms of increased profits for shareholders, or for future investment, and some will emerge in the form of increased core competencies. But a third part will remain intrinsically dependent upon the continuance of the alliance and will form a strong bonding factor. For example, economies of scale and, to some extent, of scope would be difficult to realize by the partners separately, however adept their competence internalization. There may be joint patents and designs, and frequently joint development of assets of a tangible or intangible nature which live naturally within the alliance and are not subject to individual appropriation. In addition, over time and with evolution, the alliance as an entity will begin to develop a structure of its own—and this

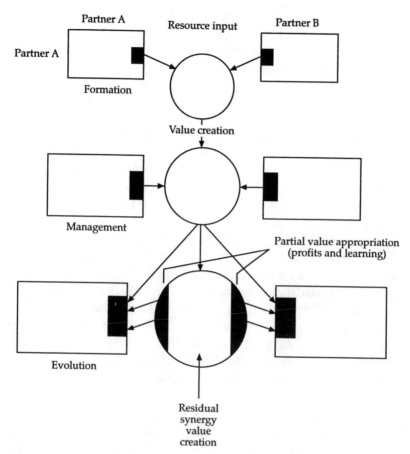

Figure 3.1 Evolution through value creation and appropriation

will be even more evident in the joint venture form of alliance.

Alliance theory proposes that conditions for evolution include:

- perception of balanced benefits from the alliance by both partners
- the development of strong bonding factors
- the regular development of new projects and responsibilities between the partners
- the adoption of a philosophy of constant learning by the partners.

BASIC RULES FOR A SUCCESSFUL ALLIANCE

To survive and be regarded as successful, alliances need to be created in a set of circumstances conducive to their development. They also need to operate in accordance with a set of basic rules, of which the following are commonly recommended in the literature. Taucher (1988) suggests that the best chance of success for an alliance is when a joint venture is concluded and the partners actively encourage the new company to develop a clear self-sustaining existence, even to the extent of encouraging flotation on the stock exchange and new additional shareholders. He cites Unilever as a good example of such a development.

Lynch (1990) suggests that the alliance should operate in the spirit of trust, co-operation and integrity, since an atmosphere of mutual distrust and domination by one partner jeopardizes the stability of the alliance. He adds two more rules for success; namely, that strategic and operational synergy prevail, and that, as the alliance matures, the partners be willing to be flexible enough to allow the structure to transform as strategic and operational conditions change. This is supported by Bleeke and Ernst (1991):

> Alliance managers should ... be prepared to rebalance the alliance—or exit smoothly—when it gets into trouble. Meeting the requirements of change, after all, is the main requirement for success in alliances.

A formula for termination should be built into the initial agreement as reassurance for both parties. If the alliance is to be successful, some clearly defined goals should be set, sufficient resources should be contributed, and the limits of the alliance should be recognized.

All commentators are clear about the major pitfalls that attend alliances that have been inadequately considered. The most important of these are:

- future conflicts due to the differing agenda of the partners;

- inadequate partner rapport leading to misunderstandings;
- fear during technology transfer that a future competitor is being created;
- cultural incompatibility;
- lack of commitment by the partners as personnel are seconded for two years then rotated.

A further risk occurs when there is a change to the strategic condition and objectives of the partners, which is not reflected in the arrangement of the alliance. This was a major factor leading to the failure of the alliance between Olivetti and AT&T.

SUMMARY

This chapter has developed the building blocks for the discussion and investigation of alliances that will be used in this book. They will be considered from the viewpoint of three phases: their set-up or formation, their subsequent management, and the degree to which they evolve into a third phase that takes them beyond the expectations that existed at the time of their formation. It then discussed certain basic rules that are commonly advocated for running alliances, both in terms of partner attitudes and organizational and structural factors. These rules will be developed further as the book progresses, and the importance of the rules will be tested against the real-life experience of existing alliances.

The following chapters deal with the three phases in the development of an alliance, and illustrate these phases through detailed historical case studies of alliances that are currently operating.

4 The formation of an alliance

The form of an alliance is one of the first issues to be addressed, once the prospective partners have agreed to embark upon a collaborative relationship. Strangely, very little of the voluminous and ever-increasing literature on alliances focuses on choice of form. Internal and external driving forces for alliances are discussed extensively, as are basic motivations and theories on why alliances are appropriate methods of meeting environmental challenges, and, to some degree, the underlying factors that are likely to make the alliances effective. However, the factors that influence the choice of form are not widely addressed. Porter and Fuller (1986) dismiss the matter as being dependent mainly on the personal preferences of the principals. Gupta and Singh (1991) are more analytic, and identify such matters as separability and specificity of assets, ease of measurement of their use, and the potential appropriability of value added, as factors that influence the type of alliance selected.

It is evident that different structural situations require the preferred use of different forms of alliance, and in this chapter specific propositions are set up to investigate this area.

SELECTION OF ALLIANCE FORM

Joint ventures

The most popular alliance is the joint venture, but which form of joint venture is most appropriate for given situations?

It is suggested that a strategic alliance should be set up as a separate joint venture company if:

(a)   the alliance scope constitutes a distinct business;
(b)   the alliance assets are
 (i)   specific,
 (ii)   easily separable from the parents,
 (iii)   need to be jointly managed;
(c)   the alliance objectives can be clearly measured in relation to the use of the assets;
(d)   there is a perceived need to commit the partners;
(e)   it is legally necessary, e.g. to gain entry to the market of another country;
(f)   the partners wish to allocate a predetermined level of resources to the venture.

In the case studies in this book, four alliances adopted the two-partner joint venture form:

1.   Dowty Group and Sema Group, with their joint venture Dowty–Sema.
2.   Eurobrek.*
3.   ICI and Enichem, with their joint venture European Vinyls Corporation, EVC.
4.   ICI Pharmaceuticals and Sumitomo Chemicals, with their joint venture, ICI Pharma.

It is clearly not sufficient to consider these cases purely to pose the question: 'Did they have the characteristics identified in the propositions, and therefore implicitly were these factors influential in determining the choice of the joint venture form?' It should also be questioned whether the choice of this form seems to have been wise, with the advantage of hindsight.

All the executives interviewed in the four ventures took the view that the bounds of the venture described a distinct business that could, if necessary, be divested in the future,

---

* This is a fictitious company name adopted to respect a confidelity agreement with the venture partners, which are known as UKCO and USCO in the text.

that the assets needed to be jointly managed, that the partners wished to commit each other to the venture, and that the achievement of the objectives set for the alliance could be clearly measured in relation to the use of the assets. These factors were, however, not very useful in predicting alliance effectiveness. When asked in the questionnaire whether the most appropriate form had been adopted, the respondents in the four joint ventures in question gave mixed replies. Only the ICI Pharma respondents answered clearly that this was the case. Generally, however, in the statistical analysis the overall preponderance of respondents claimed that the correct form had been adopted.

The alliances diverged considerably in their mode of adoption of the joint venture form. The ease of separation of the assets from the partner businesses was not so clear. Dowty–Sema was set up as a 'front office' joint venture, with the projects, when won, being 90 per cent subcontracted to the partner companies. Dowty–Sema thus had no specific assets, few central staff, and its success depended on winning Ministry of Defence contracts rather than on making profits, although it was hoped that profits would be made for the partner companies. If it were not for the wishes of the MOD, the relationship between Dowty and Sema might have been better served by a collaboration. Since it was based on a cereals business bought from Rank Hovis McDougall, Euro-brek owned assets, which included factories, staff and product brand names, but it relied for its salesforce and for a number of support services—e.g. personnel, legal and pensions—on its British-based shareholders, and this dependence (enforced by the shareholders) caused some lowering of morale within the company. EVC were forced to buy 90 per cent of their raw materials from their shareholders and even the manufacture of their commodity end-product, principally PVC, was carried out at plants that were still owned and controlled by the shareholder companies, ICI and Enichem. ICI Pharma was also a long way from being a distinct self-supporting Japanese-based pharmaceutical business. ICI provided the product specification, and the products were manufactured and, to some extent, distributed in the factories of the other partner, Sumitomo Chemical.

Thus, although an important reason in all cases for choosing the joint venture form was undoubtedly the potential to build a separate business, the partners were not wholly consistent in their decisions in supporting this objective when it came to separating the assets and assigning them to the joint venture to use exclusively in the pursuit of their objectives. In fact it could be argued that by failing to endow the ventures with their own assets in any clear manner, they lost an important part of the advantage of the joint venture form. This may well be why the alliance executives were so reluctant to confirm that the correct alliance form had been chosen.

Collaborations

The case studies of collaborative alliances were:

1. Rover and Honda
2. ICL and Fujitsu
3. Imperial Tobacco and Henri Wintermans
4. Courtaulds Coatings and Nippon Paint
5. The Royal Bank of Scotland and Banco Santander.

The idea to be tested was that the collaborative alliance form is appropriate for an alliance if:

(a) there is high uncertainty as to what tasks will be involved in the co-operative enterprise;
(b) there is a great need for flexibility between the partners;
(c) visible commitment by the partners is not sought;
(d) the boundaries of the alliance do not circumscribe a distinct business area.

Of the supporting conditions for the proposition on choice of the collaborative form of alliance, only the identification of the need to retain flexibility in the relationship received unanimous support. Only Rover/Honda and ICL/Fujitsu agreed that their initial uncertainty of what the relationship might involve prevented them from setting up a joint venture and inclined them towards the collaborative form. It is noticeable, however, that equity has been exchanged in both cases, which has the effect of cementing the relationships, and giving a sign of permanency to both employees and the market. In fact Fujitsu has bought a major share of ICL, while declaring its firm intention to continue to treat the British company as a partner rather than as a subsidiary, and to place a substantial tranche back on the market in the medium-term future.

In the case of Imperial/Wintermans, Courtaulds/Nippon Paint and RBS/Santander there were specific reasons why joint ventures were not felt appropriate for the overall relationships. In the Imperial/Wintermans case the contract was somewhat ad hoc, and certainly did not cover an area that lent itself to a joint venture. Imperial agreed to aim to achieve agreed market share targets in selling Wintermans' cigars in the UK, and Wintermans agreed to help Imperial update their production technology. Courtaulds' alliance with Nippon had the objective of having a strong representative in Japan. A joint venture in that territory would have meant a conflict of interest for Nippon, as it would have sold its products in competition with the joint venture.

Finally the RBS/Santander alliance is very complex, and was concluded at top management level to cover the whole business area of both banks, but with a requirement that both remain independent. In those circumstances only sub-projects could have been tackled in a joint venture fashion, and indeed a number of such sub-projects have been carried out.

In general, the collaborative form seems to be preferred when the partners wish to form an alliance that covers their core businesses, when the extent of the relationship is not clear at the outset, and when flexibility is essential but there is a strong requirement to retain independent identities. It is notable in the questionnaire responses from the collaboration executives in the case studies, that there is virtually total agreement that the correct alliance form was chosen. This is presumably since it is difficult to consider a well-developed complex collaboration between partners, and imagine it in another probably more constraining form. Given that Rover and Honda, for example, manufacture each other's models in their respective factories, have joint design teams, carry out research together and source components jointly, it is difficult to see how a bounded joint venture could be specified to cover all these joint activities, and also retain sufficient flexibility for future developments.

Consortia

In the case studies considered, the consortium form was adopted only by Cable and Wireless and its Japanese partners. For this alliance form, the conditions proposed as being most appropriate were:

(a) if two partners alone cannot realistically provide sufficient resources to meet the identified challenge or opportunity;
(b) if large size is necessary for the enterprise to be credible to potential customers, e.g. governments;
(c) if the specialist skills required are so wide and varied that they could not be provided adequately by two companies;
(d) if extensive geographical coverage is needed to achieve strong market presence;
(e) if there is the need to spread and limit the financial risk to each partner.

The Cable and Wireless consortium was set up in Japan in its special way because first and foremost, it would have had no hope of getting the licence to be the second international telecommunications company in Japan unless it had a range of major respected Japanese corporate partners. Even with those partners, the political battle for the licence was not easy. The Japanese partners gave it the size and importance to be credible to the Japanese government. Also, Cable and Wireless would not have had sufficient resources to tackle the opportunity with only one partner. It achieved 16 per cent of the market largely because it had 23 major Japanese partners of the importance of Toyota and C. Itoh, who of course put all their international business through the telecommunications network of which they were shareholders.

The other conditions in the proposition—namely, the need for wide specialist skills, for extensive geographical coverage, and for a limitation to the level of investment—clearly could apply as motivators for the selection of the consortium form. However, in the specific instance of the Cable and Wireless consortium these were not identified as the key conditions. Wide scope and scale are general conditions that lead to consortia formations, but to determine workable boundaries a joint venture company is normally created to provide focus and management direction. In the Cable and Wireless consortium, this company is International Digital Communications (IDC).

In the statistical sample the most important reason cited for choosing a consortium form was that the challenge was too large to be undertaken by only two partners. The next most important reasons cited were: (a) to be large enough to have credibility and (b) to achieve wide geographical coverage.

MOTIVATION

Prior to the selection of an alliance form, the prospective partners need to have a strong motivation to implement the alliance. What are the principal types of motivation?

Resource dependency

One aspect of motivation normally stems from a feeling of internal need and a sense of vulnerability. Such needs will vary in nature, but all are normally able to be classified as feelings of specific resource, skills or competence inadequacy or imbalance. Such an imbalance may be exhibited in surplus production capacity or in skill deficiency.

Each of the partners is likely to seek a different resource or skill compensation from the other. Unless both are able to match their resource or competence requirements in a particular partner, they do not have the correct partner. Their options are then to seek a different partner, or to purchase the skill from the proposed partner, but without providing a complementary skill in return. In this case the deal will be a unilateral exchange and not an alliance. Clearly, any skill imbalance relevant to a given environmental opportunity or challenge is sufficient motivation for the creation of an alliance, and no specific compensating skill or resource is necessary. All the alliances investigated were able to identify certain factors under this heading. There is also no particular reason to suppose that strong motivation for creating an alliance would be a good predictor of ultimate alliance success.

Rapidly changing technology of a global nature was a factor in the resource needs of at least one partner in seven of the ten alliances studied. Only EVC, ICI Pharma and RBS did not identify technology as an important internal motivating force. The reputation of the partner was an internal motivation in all ten alliances, coupled with access to new and strong brand names in four. This would suggest a difficulty in forming an effective alliance for companies without either a well-established reputation or strong brand names. Other factors that applied as motivations for the ten alliances studied were: local knowledge (7), marketing skills (7) and distribution channels (8).

Of other possible resource needs, key labour skills of one type or another were declared as motivating needs for Eurobrek, ICI Pharma and Cable and Wireless; and in six alliances the partner's managerial skills were stated to be the attraction. The EVC and Imperial/Wintermans alliances were attracted by at least one of the partner's access to raw materials, and Cable and Wireless identified legal requirements as their basic need in seeking to ally with a consortium of major Japanese corporations. In general, for an alliance to be formed it is clear that a mutual resource dependency perception of some sort is the key internal motivator, and that all partners are likely to have different but complementary resource requirements that they believe their chosen partner can help them to meet. The specific nature of the resource dependencies will of course be contingent on specific circumstances.

In the statistical analysis of resource dependency needs, the breadth of motivational factors were equally great. Again, 'reputation of the partner' was the factor most frequently mentioned, with technology and know-how needs, access to distribution channels, local knowledge, and access to strong brand names all being cited as key motivating forces by over two-thirds of the respondents.

Spreading financial risk

The spreading of financial risk is frequently quoted as a fundamental motivation for the formation of a strategic alliance. It seems also intuitively likely that a company with only moderate financial resources may deal with either an opportunity or a defensive challenge by seeking an alliance with a partner who can help spread the financial risk. However, of the cases studied, only Eurobrek, Fujitsu and RBS identified this as a key motive behind their alliances. The major reason may be that the alliances selected all involve substantial companies, and this may also be a powerful motive for more modestly sized companies. However, in the qualitative research carried out on the 10 alliances selected, it was, perhaps surprisingly, not generally seen as a major factor. In the 67 'statistical' alliances it was cited as a motivation by only 52 per cent of respondents—which is by no means a very high rating in importance, but is still substantial.

Fast to market

Undoubtedly an alliance represents one of the fastest means of achieving market presence to meet an opportunity if, combined, the partners have strong resources and competencies but, individually, cannot achieve critical mass in their chosen markets. Internal development would take much longer, and acquisition has the disadvantage of the possible demotivating effect of the subsidiary relationship, the higher level of investment required, and the risk of buying an unknown quantity, possibly at a premium price.

Of the 10 case studies, eight claimed speed to market as an

important motivating factor in alliance formation. For Dowty–Sema the challenge was to mount a competitive alternative to Ferranti and others in time to tender for MOD contracts. For Eurobrek it was to mount an effective challenge to Kelloggs in the UK breakfast cereals market within less than two years—a task quite impossible for the partners alone. ICI Pharma claimed that the Sumitomo alliance enabled it to get a noticeable presence on the Japanese pharmaceutical market much more quickly than could have been achieved by any other method. For Fujitsu the ICL alliance brought the Japanese company instantly into the UK and Europe as an effective force, as did the Rover alliance for Honda. For Courtaulds, the major motivator was to find a quality Japanese representative, but undoubtedly, having found one in Nippon Paint, Courtaulds were able to develop their Japanese business much faster than they had been able to previously by relying on their own resources. The alliance of the RBS and Banco Santander immediately made two smallish national banks into a medium-sized European financial enterprise, with sufficient reputation to attract other banks to its international funds transfer IBOS system. Finally, Cable and Wireless claimed speed to market as a motivator for seeking powerful Japanese allies, but in their case the allies were the passport to acceptance. It could not have been done alone.

In the statistical sample this factor attracted a rating of 78 per cent, but interestingly was negatively correlated with alliance effectiveness. This may suggest that the perceived need to enter the market quickly may lead to a rash choice of partner. However, such conjecture is not statistically justified, as the negative association with alliance effectiveness is not at a statistically significant level.

Low costs

The question of low costs as a motivator for alliance formation was interpreted to mean: 'Did you regard the alliance route as the least costly way of achieving your objectives, and if so was this a positive motivation?' In this sense, the Eurobrek, EVC, Cable and Wireless, Rover, Fujitsu, Courtaulds and RBS alliances were considered to be of relatively low cost when compared with acquisitions, and probably also with internal development; this was an important and attractive feature, but the question tended to elide with that of risk sharing.

In the statistical analysis 70 per cent of respondents cited the least cost factor overall as a motivating force for their alliance. However, this factor showed no significant statistical association with alliance effectiveness. To gain statistical support for the 'natural selection' argument that only the lowest cost organizational form would survive, the opposite results might be expected, i.e. low citation as a motivating force, but high association with alliance effectiveness through the efficiency route.

EXTERNAL FORCES

It is generally accepted that for alliances to form, some type of external driver needs to be present. Of course the specific external driver will vary from situation to situation. The most common suggested external driving forces for alliance formation are:

(a)   turbulence in markets;
(b)   economies of scale and/or scope;
(c)   globalization of the industry;
(d)   regionalization of the industry;
(e)   fast technological change leading to ever-increasing investment requirements;
(f)   shortening product life-cycles;
(g)   high economic uncertainty.

As with internal factors, any strong external factor impelling firms towards alliance formation is probably sufficient, without any one specific factor being necessary in itself. As conditions to support the proposition, seven of the more popular factors were identified and proposed to interviewees as possible external drivers. The answers varied widely. Only

Rover/Honda claimed that all the identified factors were important external drivers, and ICL/Fujitsu identified all except economic turbulence in their markets. However, if the questions had been posed at a later date this factor would probably have been included, given the current turbulent state of the world computer market.

The most common external factor identified was, perhaps not surprisingly, globalization of markets, followed closely by perceived opportunities for economies of scale and/or scope, and by the development of fast technological change. All three factors were emphasized by Eurobrek, Rover/Honda, ICL/Fujitsu, and Courtaulds/Nippon Paint. It is noteworthy that in the extended statistical sample, economies of scale and/or scope, and globalization were also dominant and that both were strongly associated with alliance effectiveness.

These factors are consistent with the most common explanation of the rapid growth of alliances in recent years. It takes the following form:

> Technology change has become increasingly rapid, and global in nature. As a result of this the difference between markets in different parts of the world has become smaller. Globalization of markets has given major opportunities for companies to realize economies of scale and scope. These factors have lowered unit costs for those firms large enough to take advantage of them. However, a side effect of technological change and globalization has been short-ening product life-cycles, leading to ever-increasing invest-ment demand both to install the new technology and to develop new products. Competitive advantage has there-fore gone to the company able to adopt the new technolo-gies, achieve economies of scale and scope, serve global markets, and change its product range regularly. Since few companies have the resources and competencies to meet these stringent requirements, there has been a widespread resort to strategic alliances to meet the needs of the new economic order.

While all of the alliances investigated have not yielded clear evidence to support this argument, a significant number have done so. EVC, Cable and Wireless, Rover/Honda, ICL/ Fujitsu and Courtaulds/Nippon Paint are all affected by the globalization of their markets. The PVC market has become increasingly global making scale economies, high-capacity utilization and consequent low unit costs crucial if EVC is to be able to compete with powerful US and Far East competitors. However, technology change and short product life-cycles are not yet important in this market. Cable and Wireless operates in the strongly global telecommunications market. This market is driven by technology change, and if Cable and Wireless is to succeed it needs the resources of a major global player. A strategy of alliances is therefore the natural route, even where such alliances do not show a short-term profit. This is the entry fee to being taken seriously in a global market. Rover/Honda operates in the global automobile market and needs to have resources, competencies and market access of the major car manufacturers if it is to succeed.

A similar argument applies to ICL/Fujitsu, although with the interesting slant that Fujitsu believes the alliance route gives competitive advantage over the large integrated company with its bureaucratic costs and single view. IBM's recent internal restructuring from a unitary hierarchy to a federal structure gives some credence to the growing currency of this view. Courtaulds Coatings and Nippon Paint's alliance is restricted to the marine paint market, where globalization and technology change are key factors, but so is market access, and this made Nippon attractive to Courtaulds.

Thus in five of the ten case study alliances the global markets and technologies paradigm provides a strong external driving force. However, the other cases are driven by other forces. Dowty–Sema was set up with the tacit encouragement of the MOD to provide a credible alternative tenderer to Ferranti for contracts in the naval command and control systems market. This market is highly specialized, and the MOD wished to deal with one additional tenderer with access to specialist skills and resources. Eurobrek operates in the mature (at least in the UK and the USA) low-technology breakfast cereals market. The external forces here are the ambition of the alliance partners to provide a strong alternative to Kelloggs, the dominant market leader. A question mark must be whether such ambition is backed by any real competitive advantage. The Imperial/Wintermans alliance had none of the conventional primary external drivers. The tobacco market is in decline, and the alliance had as a major purpose the transformation of arm's-length competitors with a distribution agreement linking them to partners able to deal more to their mutual advantage with such a market. This they have done by technology improvement and brand rationalization.

Finally, RBS and Santander have formed an alliance not because banking is becoming a global business but because the EC single market provisions threaten to regionalize the business in due course. The alliance is therefore motivated by the perceived need to be at least of a size to meet minimum critical mass requirements to attract an adequate portfolio of multinational customers in the medium-term future.

The key external forces behind international strategic alliances seem to be, as conventionally understood, the globalization of markets and technologies, the shortening of product life-cycles and the consequent need for enterprises large enough to take advantage of scale and scope economies and to afford access to adequate resources and competencies. Other factors do, however, exist in specific situations and are less generalizable in nature, but, like the internal motivations, they relate in the main to perceived resource or competency imbalances in the face of the external challenges. As with the internal factors there is no strong reason to expect a significant association between the external factors impelling a firm to seek an alliance and the ultimate effectiveness of that endeavour, although statistically both globalization and scale/scope economies are in fact so associated in the statistical sample.

PARTNER SELECTION CRITERIA

The key criteria for partner selection are most commonly suggested to be:

(a)   complementary assets;
(b)   the existence of synergies between the companies;
(c)   approximate balance in size and strength;
(d)   compatible cultures.

While there may be strong internal and external forces driving a firm towards concluding an alliance in the pursuit of competitive advantage in its market, the selection of an appropriate partner is a vital decision that may well have considerable influence on the ultimate effectiveness of the alliance. It is proposed that the above four key conditions are important considerations in such a decision. Complementary assets need not imply different types of assets, or that a partner with similar assets, e.g. factories with similar technologies, is an inappropriate partner. Assets may be complementary in type; if they are similar in nature they may still give rise to economies of scale or scope.

In the 10 case studies, complementary assets were identified by nine alliances as an important factor influencing the choice of partner. The exception was RBS and Banco Santander and this was probably because the question was interpreted as meaning complementary in the sense of 'different'. Ensuing synergies were also identified by all ten sets of partners as the key factors influencing choice of partner. Thus, Dowty provided hardware skills and Sema software skills in the defence market. USCO provided brand names and cereal marketing skills, while UKCO provided the salesforce (perhaps unnecessarily) and the joint acquisition, RHM cereals the production capacity. In EVC, both ICI and Enichem provided raw materials, capacity to make plastic and an agreement to relate that capacity more closely to market demand, i.e. by closing the least economic plants. ICI provided registered pharmaceutical products and Sumitomo provided legal access to the Japanese market together with production capacity to manufacture the product. Rover and Honda merged their activities on a number of fronts outside marketing and sales, but, at base, Rover provided access to the EC and styling competence, while Honda provided engine design and production quality skills. ICL provided access to the UK and Europe and Fujitsu provided quality, a world name and financial resources. Imperial provided market access to the UK market, and Wintermans provided modern technology skills and systems. Courtaulds provided patented product and the world's leading name in marine paint, and Nippon provided market access to Japan. RBS and Santander each provided the market presence of a medium-sized national bank with a full range of banking competencies, plus the ambition to become a strong regional enterprise, but in their view no fundamentally complementary assets. Finally Cable and Wireless provided the telecommunications expertise, while its Japanese partners provided Japanese credibility, ad hoc specialist skills, market demand for the consortium's products and influence with the Japanese ministry.

Thus, while a feeling of resource deficiency may be a dominant motivating force in alliance formation, the actual partner selection is probably more likely to have an impact on the effectiveness of the alliance. If the resource needs of the partners are not complementary, of course, they are probably best met by acquisition or internal development. Thus, if a company needs market access it must not only find a partner that can supply the necessary access, but that partner must also require something in return, e.g. technology or product, if an alliance is to follow.

The other two conditions for selection are less universally supported by the research. Alliances are not always set up between firms of similar size. However, as Killing (1983) suggests, major size mismatches may cause problems, but they may also lead to higher profits if the larger partner gives leadership. The larger partner may treat the smaller cavalierly, and the smaller partner may become over-dependent. The inevitable bureaucracy of a large company with salaried executives may co-operate uneasily with a flexible small company with shareholder executives. However, as Fujitsu seem to be demonstrating this need not be the case.

Seven of the alliances were in fact between companies of similar size, even if not of similar current strength. Even the Rover/Honda alliance, when it was formed in 1989, was between two similarly sized groups, although Honda has since tripled in size and Rover has contracted to its more profitable core. Of those alliances judged to be the most dynamic, two—namely, Rover/Honda and ICL/Fujitsu—have a stronger partner, i.e. Honda and Fujitsu.

Of the remaining three alliances all were between substantial companies. Sumitomo Chemical may not have been as large as ICI in the pharmaceutical industry, but as part of the powerful Sumitomo Group it was certainly a company of like stature. In the Cable and Wireless consortium, the numerous partners obviously varied in size but, generally, they all needed to be of high reputation and stature to perform their role effectively. Only the ICL/Fujitsu alliance is clearly unbalanced in terms of partner size and strength. Fujitsu is the second largest computer company in the world after IBM, while ICL was a struggling UK computer manufacturer with a chequered record. Fujitsu subsequently acquired 80 per cent of ICL's equity, and although declaring its intention to place a substantial tranche back on the market within four years, it still remains in a dominant position in relation to its UK partner. The fact that it has not exercised its dominance by making ICL a subsidiary is a question of policy, not capacity.

The culture condition is interesting. The question addresses the issue of whether the partners used a perceived compatible culture, however defined, as a criterion in partner selection. There is much evidence to suggest that failed alliances cite incompatibility, i.e. perhaps incompatible cultures, as a key reason for failure. Dunlop/Pirelli and AT&T/Olivetti are two well-known illustrations of this factor. However, of the ten alliances, only four identified a compatible culture as a selection criterion. These four were Eurobrek, ICL/Fujitsu, Imperial/Wintermans and RBS/Santander. It should be noted that these alliances identified the culture criterion as important. This does not mean that the cultures were in fact necessarily compatible; in fact, in the interviews, doubts were cast on the long-term compatibility of the Eurobrek partners. The other six alliances did not use cultural compatibility as a criterion. The cultures of the Dowty Group and the Sema Group are undoubtedly different, and this may have been partly responsible for many of the internal problems that emerged in the joint venture. ICI has a strong British and self-absorbed culture and finds it difficult, consequently, to operate easily in alliances with other major companies. The weaknesses in both the relationship between the partners of the joint venture EVC, and between ICI and Sumitomo in the ICI Pharma venture seem to stem from this cultural problem. Courtaulds underestimated the culture issue when forming an alliance with Nippon Paint, and the problems and existing limitations of that alliance seem to have resulted from cultural misunderstandings. In the Cable and Wireless consortium culture played no part in partner selection. Cable and Wireless has shown itself to be very aware of the cultural differences when playing a leading part in a consortium dominated by Japanese partners and based in Japan. Finally, the Rover/Honda alliance was concluded without making culture a criterion for partner selection, and this caused problems in the initial years of the partnership. Since culture has been on the agenda, however, and the partners have become ever more attuned to each other's cultural reactions to situations, the synergies developed in the alliance have grown rapidly.

The subject of partner selection criteria may be better approached from the qualitative than the statistical angle, since this enables the detail in the case to indicate whether or not real synergies and complementarities were present and whether the partners were culturally compatible. In the statistical analysis virtually all respondents claimed asset complementarity and the recognition of potential synergies as key partner selection criteria, yet there was no statistically significant association between this and the perceived effectiveness of the alliances. The most plausible reason for this is probably that the respondents felt asset complementarity and synergies to be the fundamental rationale for alliances in general, and therefore cited them. Here the limitations of questionnaire research is evident, as to perceive a potential synergy does not imply its realization in the history of the alliance.

SUMMARY

The motivations for setting up alliances seem to be created principally by feelings of resource and skill inadequacy in the face of the challenges presented by an increasingly global market affording economies of scale and scope but requiring ever higher investment. Clearly globalization of markets and technologies is a key factor at this point in history. It is, of course, in an overall sense only a special case for determining alliances. The general motivating case can be stated in the form:

> *If the skill and resources are perceptibly less than those required to meet a challenge or opportunity most effectively, and the prospective partners appear to be able to supply each other's deficiencies, then there is a motivation to form an alliance to supplement those skills and resources.*

Thus firms tend to seek a partner whom they perceive to have complementary assets from which synergies can be realized. They prefer firms of similar size and stature in order to minimize the risk of domination, excessive dependence and an equitable balance of benefits. They do not so frequently consider compatible cultures as key criteria in partner selection, but the extent to which this aspect of a potential partner is ignored increases the probability of future inter-organizational problems. The choice of alliance form may be weakly influenced by circumstances—e.g. joint ventures for distinct non-core businesses, collaborations for core businesses and consortia for situations demanding size—but the logic of the choice is often not followed through in appropriate organizational arrangements, and this manifestly reduces the benefits of appropriate form selection.

Chapters 5 and 6 describe case studies from the viewpoint of the formation of the alliance.

5 The Cable and Wireless consortium

This chapter describes the formation of the Japanese telecommunications consortium led by Cable and Wireless plc. In 1985 Cable and Wireless (C&W), the British-based telecommunications group, decided to attempt to increase its prominence in the fast globalizing telecommunications industry by putting together a consortium to bid for an international telecommunications licence in Japan. After a long series of negotiations with potential Japanese partners, the consortium was formed, and in October 1986 C&W, C. Itoh, Toyota, Pacific Telesis plus 13 smaller Japanese 'sleeping' shareholders announced their bid for the licence, through a consortium company, International Digital Communications (IDC). This followed considerable nationalistic opposition from the Japanese government, which did not want to see a major foreign company in a leading position in its international telecommunications industry. The then British Prime Minister, Mrs Thatcher, told her then Japanese counterpart, Yasuhiro Nakasone, that she regarded UK participation in the new service as a test of Japan's willingness to open its markets. Ultimately, IDC was given the licence.

THE JAPANESE TELECOMS INDUSTRY

As in the British telecoms industry, the 1980s brought privatization to the Japanese industry. Nippon Telephones and Telegraph (NTT) was privatized in 1984, and is the dominant domestic telecoms company in Japan. It is, however, prohibited at present from operating internationally. There are three domestic competitors to NTT in Japan, including DDI and NKT with whom C&W initially tried to form an alliance. At that time this was thwarted by the chauvinism of the Japanese Ministry of Telecommunications and Posts.

In the international Japanese market the dominant Japanese company is Kokusai Denshin Denwa (KDD), the privatized ex-monopolist. However, the two other companies whose growing strength is proving effective in keeping prices competitive are International Telecoms Japan (ITJ) and International Digital Communications (IDC)—i.e. the C&W consortium. KDD is estimated to have 68 per cent of the market (from 100 per cent five years ago), with ITJ and IDC having 16 per cent each. The Japanese international telecoms market is estimated to be worth more than £2.5 billion by 1995.

CABLE AND WIRELESS

C&W has been in existence for over 120 years, and has a presence in over 50 different countries of the world. Despite this longevity and global spread, it is not yet a global giant, being dominated in the UK by British Telecom in the corporate and personal markets. In 1991 it had a relatively modest sales turnover of £2.5 billion, and pre-tax profits of £600 million.

Since the privatization of the British telecommunications industry, the Cable and Wireless Group has set itself the objective of becoming a leader in the world industry, as spreading privatization makes more and more of the world's telecoms systems available to private enterprise operators.

C&W has a considerable range of activities, all within the telecoms industry. In the UK it owns Mercury Communications which is set to compete with BT for the personal and corporate UK consumer in the 1990s. Currently it pays interconnection charges to BT to operate on the BT network, but, conscious that this leaves it very vulnerable to its rival, it is in the process of developing wireless access for its customers to by-pass the BT network. Through Mercury

Personal Communications it hopes to develop a leading role in the fast-growing PCN market. It operates the Hong Kong telecoms network, and is fast establishing a presence in most Far East markets by acquisition, franchise or alliance. It also views Europe and the USA as important markets to conquer, and has a number of activities both individually and by joint venture operating in these territories. It has been instrumental in building the Global Digital Highway, a broad-band fibre optic network connecting the main business and commercial centres of Europe, North America and the Pacific Rim. The last major section, the North American cable, was brought into service in 1991.

Operation in Japan is considered to be a long-term involvement in which the only way to function successfully is to put down roots and relate sympathetically with the Japanese culture and method of doing business. Cable and Wireless's approach therefore involves co-operative strategies, and in this respect it has been the driving force in IDC. The Japanese consortium won the Japanese licence to provide a second Japanese international carrier. C&W also set up a joint venture Fair-Way Networks taking it into the Japanese domestic market for the first time, and strengthening its capability in data networking.

C&W considers the fast-changing global market to be to its advantage, and in the words of its chairman Lord Young it is 'Continuing to evolve as a worldwide service provider' with the now well-established principle of acting locally but thinking globally.

FORMATION OF THE CONSORTIUM

If C&W wished to bid for a Japanese telecoms licence, it had no option but to form a joint venture with a Japanese partner. However, there were a number of options within this alliance form: for example, they could have chosen to form a joint venture with one major Japanese telecoms company, with C&W providing the international experience; or they could have formed a more flexible collaborative relationship, or set of relationships.

The form they chose was a consortium joint venture. This was stimulated by the size necessary to achieve credibility with the Japanese government. Other criteria, such as complementary skills, were not the prime determinants, and in many respects the partners are something of a miscellany of major corporations, in many cases without any obvious existing experience in telecoms. This reflects very largely the way they were recruited. Their differing internal agendas may also possibly not bode well for the ultimate future of IDC. However, by spreading the shareholding widely, and by being the dominant telecoms expert, C&W has probably achieved a position of more influence in a foreign theatre than could have been achieved if a partnership had been sought with only one major Japanese telecoms company. However, its position is still slightly frustrating. As Takehiro Ikeuchi, a C&W Japanese director, stated:

> The other shareholders should listen to our opinions and views more than they do, as we are the only partner with international telecoms experience. It is very difficult for us to take the initiative as we are a British company. In general the situation has not been developed with determination. For example, we set up another company in the USA owned 100 per cent by ourselves, and already the company employs 2000 staff from the same starting point. The trouble is that in Japan we need C. Itoh's 'nemawashi' [behind the scenes lobbying and consensus building particularly with the Ministry] and they have no experience of the telecoms industry.

Initially C&W established a feasibility company with C. Itoh, the major Japanese trading house, and NTT. C. Itoh introduced some major Japanese corporations, including Toyota. When IDC was eventually set up in its final form, C&W, C. Itoh and Toyota became the major partners, each with 17 per cent of the equity, making 51 per cent in total. Pacific Telesis of the USA has 10 per cent; there are eleven core members of major Japanese companies such as NEC, Nippon Steel, Fujitsu and a number of banks, and then a tail of 120 other shareholders. The wide Japanese shareholding was valuable (a) to gain credibility with the Japanese ministry and (b) to provide initial consumers. Naturally, when the shareholders make international calls they use IDC facilities, and this has helped greatly in winning market share from the outset.

Toyota's position is seen as slightly anomalous. It seems to have been reluctant to join at the outset, but having joined with 10 per cent of the equity, it took the opportunity of a rights issue to increase its shareholding to 17 per cent alongside that of C. Itoh and C&W and is very forceful, despite its lack of telecoms experience. Somewhat gnomically, Toshio Horiuchi, a Toyota seconded director of IDC, says:

> We (Toyota) do not have a clear intention as concerns the international telecoms business. However, Toyota is now making great progress in globalization, so we are one of the major customers for international telecoms; so we thought of getting into the business to represent the customer's viewpoint.

The internal motivation for the consortium was the need to put together a credible team in terms of size, technological experience and Japanese substance, to take advantage of the opportunity provided by the tender for the licence for the second international carrier. C&W provided the technology and international experience outside Japan, and the partners provided all other requirements; they are influential in the right quarters in Japan—C. Itoh is very useful in purchasing; the banks are useful with lines of credit and so forth. However, these capacities to make a contribution are more by chance than planned.

The skills of the partners are diverse. All have good general business experience, mostly in Japan; C. Itoh is a strong trading partner, Pacific Telesis is strong in telecoms but not internationally, Toyota is a very powerful name and NTT (international), although not an operating subsidiary, is technologically strong and able to provide telecoms-trained human resources. C&W is the strongest partner from the viewpoint of international telecoms experience, but is not capable of conducting *nemawashi* by itself in Japan.

The partners' objectives, however, are not necessarily congruent in the longer term. C&W has the objective of becoming established in Japan in a significant way. C. Itoh wants to expand into telecoms. Toyota want to be part of the project because it is big. NTT wants to learn the international telecoms business, possibly before becoming a competitor of C&W in any reshuffle of licences in the future. However, any conflicting agendas are dealt with at shareholder level, and do not impede the smooth running of the management team.

The alliance is rated as being successful, both internally and within the industry generally, although, as with most consortia, observers with sceptical temperaments can see possible seeds of disquiet that may grow from the fact that, for most of the partners, an alliance with C&W is not crucial once the telecoms business has been learned. Nonetheless spin-off benefits have been major, and even if the consortium were not to prove a long-term arrangement, its establishment and impact justify its rating as a success.

A key to the success of the alliance, apart from the correct mix of skills, power and influence, has been the bonding that has taken place as a result of the fight for acceptance with the Ministry of Telecommunications and Posts. As Jonathan Soloman of C&W says:

> The IDC situation was born in crisis, and lives in crisis. At the outset the resistance from the Japanese Ministry created a crisis ambience in the company, and the attempt to wrest market share from the ex-monopolist KDD means constant crisis attitudes.

An additional important factor was the choice of the consortium form, which through its multiplicity of partners, enabled C&W in one corporate strategic action to become close to a substantial number of Japanese major corporations.

The most crucial period in IDC's history was between inception and the granting of the licence. Subsequently, the management of the company has led to its successful establishment and market share acquisition, but not as yet to major remittable profits. From C&W's viewpoint this is not crucial, although it might be an important factor weighing against the investment of further large amounts of capital in the enterprise in the future. The key success objective for C&W has been establishing itself in Japan, and this seems to have been largely accomplished. Further objectives that have developed from observing the Japanese have been concerned with learning. IDC is very effective at marketing, and C&W is concerned that currently it does not seem to be able to transfer the knowledge it has gained from this to, say, Mercury; in Britain the 'Not invented here' syndrome still causes resistance.

SUMMARY

The alliance has undoubtedly been a success despite current lack of major profits to date. It has achieved a 16 per cent international market share. C&W has made strong Japanese friends, been accepted in Japan, and been able to set up a further joint venture, Fair-Way Networks, on the domestic front in Japan. Japan, which once had the highest prices in international telecoms in the Asian region, now has some of the lowest; and after not even being on the major networks of the world, it has in a few years become the major hub-centre for the whole area. Much of this is due to the stimulus provided by IDC. The capital value of IDC has increased to about 700 times its initial share value as at July 1992. Also, Mercury now has about 30 per cent of the UK traffic with Japan, which it certainly would not have had without IDC, so for the £17 million invested by C&W the spin-off benefits have been immense.

6 The Dowty–Sema joint venture

In 1982 a joint venture company called Gresham Cap was formed by Gresham Lyons and Cap Scientific software company to bid for UK Ministry of Defence naval command and control systems projects. Ten years later, after several name changes, following changes of ownership in the partner companies, the then entitled Dowty–Sema was fully absorbed into Bae–Sema, itself a joint venture of British Aerospace and the French Sema software company. The joint venture had lasted 10 years, and despite frequently changing ownership arrangements, had been very successful in gaining MOD contracts.

HISTORY OF THE INDUSTRY

The market at which the joint venture was aimed was very specialized—namely, for the supply of command and control systems for the navy, to be fitted to surface ships and submarines. These systems involve electronics equipment, including computers, software and associated interfacing equipment, that integrate the weapons and sensors that make up a naval combat system.

It is a relatively new industry, dating from the late 1960s. Prior to that, the central command and control functions of the combat systems were plotted manually. However, as sensors and weapons became more complex, and the sophistication of computers developed rapidly, a new industry of computer-assisted command and control evolved at the centre of the combat system. In effect it became the brain and central nervous system of the combat arena.

In the 1970s the industry was dominated by Ferranti, because it succeeded in developing proprietary computers customized to military use and suited to these applications. However, the industry had a chequered history as the computers were difficult to build and Ferranti was not particularly innovative.

Gresham Lyons was already in the industry at this time, as a small company providing analogue computers to solve simple fire control problems, particularly for torpedoes. Gresham Lyons was the traditional supplier in the submarine market, but was threatened by Ferranti when the first computer-based command and control system was developed, combining both sensor and weapon systems—a system called DCB. Gresham Lyons was initially the prime contractor, and Ferranti the subcontractor, providing all the software. In this way, Gresham Lyons was able to defend its position in the submarine market.

By the early 1980s, however, the market had developed further, and it had become clear that the successful bidders for contracts would be the innovators who could offer computers and associated software technology. Gresham Lyons had no expertise in these areas, and could see no long-term future in its relationship with Ferranti, as it realized that Ferranti had the capability to do the entire job. However, Gresham Lyons had long-standing experience in delivering supporting equipment in the naval environment, an understanding of the equipment with which it interfaced, and a reputation in the market, with all the contacts that that involved. It realized that to survive it needed a partner to provide the computer-related technology, and this was the beginning of Gresham Lyons' relationship with Cap Scientific.

Cap Scientific came into the market in 1979 to work in the government and defence sector, and soon established a reputation for being very innovative. In the words of Martin Davis, a project manager with Cap Scientific at the time:

Gresham Lyons did not see Cap Scientific to be a threat to their position. Gresham Lyons were good at making boxes, and Cap were a collection of people who could write software. So their skills were complementary and Gresham Cap was set up to tender for the command and control system to replace DCB.

Subsequently Gresham Lyons was bought by the Dowty Group and Cap Scientific was merged into the French-based Sema Group; the joint venture became successively Dowty–Cap and then Dowty–Sema. Sema then set up a further joint venture in 1991 with British Aerospace called Bae–Sema and transferred its 50 per cent holding in Dowty–Sema into this vehicle. Dowty was then sold to the TI Group in 1992, but the TI Group sold its 50 per cent holding in Dowty–Sema to Bae–Sema, thus making Dowty–Sema a wholly owned subsidiary of Bae–Sema in November 1992.

Thus at the ownership level the joint venture passed through many changes during its ten years of existence, but at the operational level it consistently won MOD contracts, and is prepared in the 1990s to expand globally with a bid for a contract for the Korean navy.

THE FORMATION OF DOWTY–SEMA

As Guy Warner, managing director of Dowty–Sema for much of its life, stated:

> Dowty–Sema was formed as a hardware–software joint venture. Each party brought a different skill, and of course there were two completely different cultures. Dowty was the hardware equipment supplier, which had an essentially manufacturing type of culture, and Sema was the software people-only type business. One made its money from people, the other from selling hardware.

Dowty–Sema was set up as a joint venture largely because this was felt to be the appropriate 'shop front' to present to the Ministry of Defence with a view to winning tenders against such competitors as Ferranti, Racal or Plessey.

Martin Davis, a project executive with the company, commented:

The major client, the MOD, perceived great strength in the alliance, and wouldn't have felt that either partner on their own would have had the requisite credibility.

However, the manner in which the joint venture was formed caused many operational problems, and it was difficult to make a profit since clear decision-taking and leadership could not easily be shown in a joint venture without dedicated resources, staff or profit responsibility.

The key motivation for the alliance was to gain access to lucrative MOD contracts. The partner selection was based on the presumed synergy between the two companies existing through the complementarity of their assets and core competencies; Dowty was a hardware company and Sema provided software. There was also strong encouragement from the MOD behind the scenes. Although the assets and skills of Dowty and Sema were complementary, the cultures of the two partners were definitely not. Martin Davis commented:

> A Sema person's view of a Dowty man would be of an old and bold harbour engineer, a bit fuddy duddy, not that creative, always the one to raise artificial barriers to getting something done. The corresponding opinion by a Dowty person of a Sema person would be a 25-year-old fly-by-night, with wonderful ideas but without regard for their practicality, or the reality of engineering real systems that have to be put in ships and supported. This caused great difficulty from the outset, and it continues to cause great difficulty.

The joint venture was set up essentially as a front office through which the hardware activities were to be subcontracted to Dowty and the software to Sema. So the subcontractors were to be where the real work was done, and the subcontractors could continue to live in their respective cultures. Other business functions were to be split equally, with Dowty looking after contracts and Sema after finance. The joint venture had the strong support of the MOD, since they wanted a credible competitor to Ferranti.

Dowty–Sema seems in many ways to be a collaboration between Dowty and Sema masquerading as a joint venture for the convenience of the MOD. It does not have the characteristic distinguishing aspects of a joint venture in terms of autonomy and the assets to get on with the job, and, accordingly, the organizational arrangements led to a diffusion of power at the cost of efficiency, and the consequent diminution of the ability to make profit from its contracts.

Dowty–Sema was a joint venture in which power was never given to the venture company. The partners continued to organize the venture from the wings, and to carry out 90 per cent of the contracts directly as subcontractors within their own companies, although those contracts had been won by the joint venture company. Thus, Dowty and Sema were the shareholders of the joint venture and, hence, owners and directors; but, also rather uneasily, subcontractors and, hence, clients of the joint venture company. This led to some confusion of identity on the board, and to the need for the managing director of Dowty–Sema to act more as a diplomat than a businessman. As Guy Warner commented:

> As we have become more successful we have become a threat to the subcontractor operations. The actual subcontractor organizations are divisions of the bigger entities, and report up the line to directors that sit on my board. But every bit of work they have is subcontracted from us, so they haven't been successful in diversifying out of that themselves, and this creates tension between us.

For tenders, teams were put together from the joint venture and the two partners. The executives of both partners then assisted with the implementation. The Dowty–Sema staff carried out three functions:

1.   Overall project management
2.   Systems activities that spanned both hardware and software areas
3.   Marketing and business development

Dowty–Sema does not have its own payroll or pension scheme and, at least originally, was not meant to be profit-responsible. The theory held that the staff could return to the parent companies, but Dowty–Sema has grown so rapidly that that has not happened. As Guy Warner stated: 'We have to fight to get the best people. They put them in for bids, then when the bid is won they pull them back.' Rivalry also tended to develop during bids, as members of the team saw possibilities of work for their parent organizations rather than for the joint venture.

The entry of British Aerospace has unbalanced the alliance, however, and has led indirectly to the partnership becoming a wholly owned subsidiary of a Bae–Sema joint venture. However, this will probably benefit the company, as it will now be able to overcome the errors committed at the time of its formation—that is, it was formed, with MOD encouragement, as a joint venture company but was not given the tools or the powers to develop as a self-standing entity.

SUMMARY

The joint venture has clearly been a success. From its formation in 1982, it has grown to employ more than 100 staff and have an annual turnover of £50 million. However, to quote Guy Warner:

> It hasn't been wholly a success. We've been successful at expanding the business, but the subcontractors haven't made the profit they hoped to. We took a big risk on the technology to win the submarine contract, and the implementation of that technology, especially on the software side, has cost a lot of money. You have to get three-way agreement to all decisions, so decision-making is too slow, and this has meant that they have lost money.

The TI Group, having bought Dowty, did not want to be in the defence sector, so it sold its holding in Dowty–Sema to Bae–Sema. Consequently, Dowty–Sema is now a wholly owned subsidiary of Bae–Sema, with the ex-subcontracting division of Sema as the other subsidiary. However, the Bae–Sema joint venture is run as an integrated operation, with its own payroll, pension scheme and profit responsibility, and Dowty–Sema may well prosper as a result of the transfer.

7 The management of alliances

The conditions surrounding the motivations for strategic alliances, the circumstances in which alliances are most likely to be considered, their various forms and criteria for selecting partners are all detailed extensively in the various management journals. But on the issue of how best to manage an alliance, most authors, if they deal with the subject at all, content themselves by laying out a few basic rules. As Niederkofler (1991) has stated:

> a major cause for cooperative failure is managerial behaviour. In nature, cooperation differs fundamentally from competition. Whereas competitive processes are well understood and practised daily, the key success factors in cooperative processes are widely ignored.

Yet it seems that the success of an alliance will lie more likely in its management than in the form of its initial creation. Professor Harrigan, one of the most voluminous writers on joint ventures, comments: 'Alliances fail because operating managers do not make them work, not because contracts are poorly written' (Harrigan, 1986).

However, different guidelines obviously apply to alliances that have separate joint venture companies than to complex collaborations without joint venture boundaries. In all alliance forms, however, the following considerations are involved:

1. Setting up and running appropriate systems.
2. Agreeing non-conflicting objectives.

3.   Adopting appropriate attitudes.

Teramoto *et al.* (1991), in identifying the six factors they believe to be most important for strengthening the links between companies in an alliance, focus on formation, successful results and management.

1.   The formation criterion is inevitably complementarity of resources.
2.   The results criteria are to achieve tangible benefits on both sides through reciprocal trade, and to experience early success to demonstrate the value of the alliance.
3.   The management criterion consists of three factors:
      – to identify an early target or objective for the alliance
      – to develop a close relationship on a personal basis between the partners
      – to communicate well through an effective boundary spanning function.

ORGANIZATIONAL ARRANGEMENTS

The role of the management function is clearly important, yet it is perhaps the most neglected in the planning of alliances. The systems devised to carry out the management of an alliance are crucial if the alliance is to function effectively.

Control

Control is a key aspect of alliances, if only because it is less clear than in hierarchies, and can therefore easily lead to diffusion of purpose owing to the lack of defined systems of authority. Geringer and Hebert (1989) suggest that alliance partners tend to define control in the following terms:

1.   *Focus*—the scope of activity over which they wish to exercise control.
2.   *Extent*—the degree of control they wish to exercise.
3.   *Mechanism*—how they wish to exercise control, e.g. at

board meetings, informally, or by retaining the right to make their own decisions on certain issues.

They found that joint ventures were most profitable where parent companies showed a relaxed attitude to control. This may have been because the transaction costs of building complex control systems were not deemed necessary, and the motivation of joint venture managers was thereby increased by their feelings of autonomy. Lorange and Roos (1992) take a similar view and claim that, since control must be a dynamic quality, it is a question of establishing a base for persuasion rather than being reactive with orders. Alliances depend for their decisions on building consensus between the partners, and where legal control leads to one partner short-circuiting this process by making unilateral decisions, the strength of the alliance suffers.

DISPUTE RESOLUTION MECHANISMS

Interestingly, the investigation into how disputes were resolved in alliances was the one area that showed the greatest divergence between the detailed evidence provided by the interviewees and their responses to questions related to propositions posed to them directly. For example, sensitivity to different national cultures was claimed by all interviewees, except those from Dowty–Sema, yet stories from ICI Pharma, EVC and Courtaulds suggest areas of considerable insensitivity in these alliances. Similarly, most alliances claimed to have a good dispute resolution mechanism, yet Dowty–Sema, and Rover/Honda provide evidence to suggest that these alliances sometimes had considerable problems in resolving disputes.

In general, the alliances claiming good dispute resolution mechanisms are those with joint ventures. Only Rover/Honda and RBS/Santander of the collaborations made such claims. Of course, dispute systems are easier to formulate in joint ventures, since they have clear hierarchies with a chief executive at the apex reporting to a board of directors. In those circumstances day-to-day disputes can be resolved in the normal way, as in other companies. Where disputes arise between joint venture personnel and partner company personnel, they can be resolved ultimately at joint venture board level, which almost always contains representatives of the partner companies in addition to the joint venture management.

The collaborations, ICL/Fujitsu, Imperial/Wintermans and Courtaulds/Nippon Paint admit to less than adequate dispute resolution mechanisms, and this is inevitably the alliance form with the greatest opportunity for ambiguity in this area. Yet Imperial/Wintermans and Courtaulds/Nippon Paint have adopted a form of the 'gateway' system, which gives a degree of focus to the contacts between the companies, and Fujitsu have seconded a small number of senior personnel to ICL headquarters in Putney to attend to such relationships. The 'gateway' is normally personified in a senior executive in each company who either directly manages the interfaces between the companies and hence, by implication, the disputes, or is at least informed of all such contacts. As Jose Saavedra, the 'gateway' for Banco Santander, points out, it is a good system but it should ultimately wither away as the partners form closer relationships. According to Niederkofler (1991), the mission of the 'gateway' executives is boundary-spanning:

> By limiting the actual amount of cooperation, by a careful selection of appropriate boundary spanners, and by stepping up the involvement with the partner as the firms get to know each other, the effects of organizational incompatibilities may be moderated.

Boundary-spanning is a critical aspect of alliances, and the skill with which it is carried out seems to have considerable impact on the success of the alliance.

In the statistical analysis a good dispute mechanism is seen as highly significantly associated with alliance effectiveness, and is an important factor in the process.

CLARITY OF AUTHORITY

There is again mixed experience on the clarity of authority in the hands of the managing directors of the joint ventures.

Dowty–Sema admit that such authority was not granted; consequently an inordinate amount of time was spent in meetings, with the result that projects that should have been profitable proved to be unprofitable.

The other joint ventures have claimed that clear authority was given to the managing director. However, such claimed authority did not help John York of EVC in his quest for greater independence in choosing the suppliers of his raw materials, or the managing director of Eurobrek, who could not select his own salesforce. Of the other alliances with separate joint venture companies, the C&W consortium is run as a Japanese company, so consensus rather than clear authority is the dominant culture; and this is also the pattern in ICI Pharma.

Interestingly, clarity of authority did not appear as a significant variable in the statistical tests, which does not mean that it is unimportant, but simply indicates that it is not a contentious issue.

APPROPRIATE FORM

All the alliances investigated claimed, even with the benefit of hindsight, to have adopted the most appropriate form of alliance. The key factors determining appropriate form seem to be:

- a *joint venture*, where a separate business circumscribes the logical bounds of the alliance, and the business is probably non-core;
- a *collaboration*, where the alliance is at corporate level, touches at many activity points, needs to be flexible and involves core activities;
- a *consortium*, where the project is too large for varying reasons for a two-partner alliance, and the enterprise needs to be credible to customers, especially governments.

On the basis of these criteria, the alliances do indeed seem to have chosen their alliance form wisely. However, in the case of the joint ventures, the partners have generally not carried through the separate business logic, i.e. to grant the venture the assets and authority it needs to have the best chance of being most effective. Dowty–Sema has no real assets; EVC is only now managing to acquire some; Eurobrek is not allowed its own salesforce; and ICI Pharma has no production unit. It could also be reasonably maintained that were it not for the wishes of the MOD, Dowty–Sema might have been better run as a collaboration. At all events, this operational variable was not significant in the statistical analysis. The contention might well be: the method you use to run an alliance matters more than the form you choose.

DIVORCE PROCEDURE

It is suggested by Taucher (1988) that the most comfortable alliances are those who have agreed at formation a formula for dissolving the alliance, should it be felt by either partner to be no longer of value. This seems logical, since it should reduce anxiety that a failing alliance might destroy the partners in its wake, as the ill-fated Dunlop/Pirelli alliance so nearly did. However, only Dowty–Sema, Eurobrek and EVC claimed to have dealt with such matters on their negotiating agenda. Since all the alliances investigated are still in existence, and therefore successful at least by minimal criteria, the implications of having no pre-agreed divorce formulae have not been tested. This factor does not appear as significant in the statistical analysis, but it is probably a useful issue to have on the check-list for negotiators.

INFORMATION DISSEMINATION

A further condition proposed for an appropriate organizational system is that of ensuring that information on the alliance is widely disseminated within the partner companies. This stimulates interest in the alliance and encourages its support, and also encourages the development of the increased knowledge that can always be gained through close association with another company. Of the alliances investigated, all except ICI Pharma claimed that information on the alliance was acceptably well disseminated in the partner companies. The importance of this would, of course, vary with the degree to which the alliance involved core activities or only peripheral activities of the partner companies. Most, but not all of the alliances involved core activities. Eurobrek only involves a very small part of both partner companies; EVC involves a relatively small part of ICI, but a more core part of Enichem; the Imperial/Wintermans alliance is only for cigars, which are central to Wintermans but peripheral to Imperial; and the RBS/Santander alliance affects only a small part of the staff of both banks. Where a partner is involved in a non-core activity, there is a greater onus on that partner to ensure a wide dissemination of information or there is a risk that the alliance will become of decreasing interest to the remainder of that partner's company. Rover claim that much of the benefit they have received from the Honda alliance has been through information dissemination within Rover, and the consequent organizational learning that has taken place. Jonathan Soloman of C&W bemoans the fact that C&W's subsidiary Mercury could learn a lot from the experience of IDC but does not seem sufficiently interested to do so. In the statistical analysis, information dissemination was considered to be as important as a good dispute resolution mechanism.

CONGRUENT GOALS

For smooth management of an alliance the long-term goals of the partners should obviously not be in conflict. There are two potential problems with goals: first, the underlying goals of the partners may be in conflict, but that fact may be concealed on formation, lest it abort an otherwise attractive alliance with good potential short-term advantages for both or all partners; second, the goals may be congruent at the outset, but may subsequently grow into conflict, often as a result of the success of the alliance.

Most of the alliance executives interviewed claimed that

their companies had non-conflicting goals with their partners. The exceptions were the Dowty–Sema joint venture and ICI Pharma who clearly had conflicting goals, despite their moderate measures of objective success. The problem has been resolved for Dowty–Sema with its 100 per cent acquisition by Bae–Sema. In ICI Pharma no long-term resolution has been determined, as ICI are, with Sumitomo's knowledge, setting up their own Japanese production unit into which they will take much of the profit from the activity.

The other alliances all claim compatible long-term goals. However, this is doubtful in some cases. It is suspected among Eurobrek staff that UK CO may seek to buy 100 per cent of Eurobrek in the near future. ICI's stake in EVC is probably currently on sale, if industry commentators are to be believed, and although it is clear that the development of the venture is a high priority to Enichem, ICI's priority in the area is to conserve its funds. C&W admit that their partners all have differing agendas and that the consortium cannot be expected to remain stable for ever. C&W are happy with this as their basic objective is to develop a reputation in Japan of a good corporate citizen. If this is achieved, C&W believes that new opportunities will emerge. Imperial does not have the long-term interest of Wintermans at heart, and as it now has modern technology it could easily replace Wintermans' brands with its own on the UK market. Courtaulds wants Nippon Paint to continue to be its representative in Japan. Nippon has been so successful, however, that its longer term goals have developed to make it a more global player.

Thus, of the 10 alliances, eight could realistically be considered to have possible conflicting long-term goals. Yet only Dowty–Sema and ICI Pharma admit to this. If nothing else, this demonstrates the degree to which the management of an alliance involves constant negotiation to find overlaps between goals, rather than to clarify totally congruent goals.

The potential problem of conflicting objectives is ever-present in alliances, since, perhaps, the partners wish to obtain the advantages of joint activity while retaining their individual autonomy. As individual autonomy inevitably presents the potential for the development of conflicting objectives, a substantial contribution to success must therefore depend upon the quality of 'mutual forbearance'.

In the statistical analysis the reluctance of executives to look too closely at the underlying realities in this area also displays itself. 'Congruent goals' fail to make the cut-off statistical significance level when cross-tabulated with 'alliance effectiveness'. Even relatively ineffective alliances still contend that their objectives are in line, because a declaration that they are not may herald the break-up of the alliance. It may be concluded, then, that congruent goals are indeed important, but the area is frequently left as ambiguous between the partners.

POSITIVE PARTNER ATTITUDES

Management involves more than just systems and goals however. It is critically concerned with attitudes and interpersonal relationships, and these were shown to be the most important factors in the whole investigation.

Mutual trust, commitment and cultural sensitivity

Trust and goodwill have been found to be vital in alliances of all kinds. Niederkofler (1991) states that:

> goodwill and trust were found to have a stabilizing effect on the relationship at all development stages. They increased the partners' tolerance for each others' behaviour and helped avoid conflicts. Goodwill and trust also raised the general level of communication between the partners and thereby increased the chances for uncovering and dealing with operating misfit.

Lynch (1990) emphasizes the need for partner rapport, and consequently advises that two-year secondments do not give sufficient time to build this rapport and commitment. Kanter (1989) stresses that the management of alliances requires very different attitudes and behaviour from the management of hierarchies: 'It is essential for them [managers] to be able to juggle constituencies, rather than control subordinates.'

Consensus-building replaces decision-taking, and respect in alliances comes not with rank but with knowledge and the ability to get things done, as John Bacchus of Rover stresses. Given the clear importance to all relationships—and alliances in particular—of positive and flexible attitudes, and the fact that all the alliances investigated claimed to be to some extent successful (they were after all still in existence!), it is perhaps not surprising that the interviewees claimed generally positive attitudes in relation to the alliances.

Careful analysis of the transcripts of the interviews, however, revealed a more varied picture. On the surface, nine of the ten alliances claimed to have positive attitudes on both or all sides towards national and corporate cultural differences, to have strong commitment from top management and below in the organization, and to have a high level of mutual trust. Dowty–Sema was alone in admitting that cultural sensitivities on a national and corporate level could be improved, that commitment at the top was strong but much weaker lower down the partner organizations, and that a very limited degree of mutual trust existed among those actively involved in the alliance. RBS/Santander also highlighted the less than complete commitment in their organizations, especially at local bank manager level, where the relevance of the alliance to their everyday lives was not always appreciated. For the other alliances, however, high marks were claimed for cultural sensitivity, commitment and trust. How far this mutual congratulation was justified needs to be examined more deeply.

Eurobrek is clearly regarded as a successful alliance, and is making a determined attempt to compete effectively with the market leader Kelloggs. As one of its senior executives commented:

There are debates and disagreements about how to service customers, but you would have that in a non-joint venture. Although if I had my way I would be working with the rest of the business. But I have to say the business has been very successful because each part of the business has worked better than it did before. Although some expensive lessons have been learnt on product launches.

On the question of partner attitudes he claimed:

> In (UKCO) there is a culture of arrogance. They say '(USCO) small compared with us. (USCO) is successful in the US but nowhere else.' They are saying 'We are (UKCO). We don't like partnerships, and have only done it to get our foot in the camp and we will buy out (USCO) in the fullness of time.' And there is a view here that will happen.

Thus success, at least to the end of phase one, is being achieved (the alliance is only three years old), but perhaps there is some room for development in attitudes appropriate to long-term co-operative relationships. It appears that if Eurobrek is to become a strong self-standing breakfast cereals company it will need not just market share but an acceptance by its parent companies that it should manage the assets needed to secure its future, and have access to the parents for advice rather than control.

At EVC, John York faced a task which involved the withdrawal of substantial PVC production capacity. In order to align the ICI and Enichem supply capacity in PVC to market demand, he also faced two very strong cultures. ICI have a very strong internal culture based on teamwork and debate, while Enichem are much more functionally driven. The production director at Enichem, for example, applies himself to production and is somewhat loath to express an opinion related to other areas. In ICI the concept of board member is more broadly interpreted. These different cultures could not fuse easily in EVC, and John York had some trouble over clashing cultures as a result. As he says:

> I let it [the EVC culture] evolve over a few years and we have evolved an EVC culture and style. Both shareholders are uncomfortable with it as it doesn't fit with their norms. But I think we have evolved our own culture.

While the company was making substantial profits, York no doubt had the power to do this. Recession has hit EVC, however, in the last few years, and the lack of comfort by shareholders may well have resurfaced. At least John York has now passed on the baton to a new chief executive.

The ICI Pharma relationship also seems to have met cultural problems, and in this case these problems have clearly impeded the development of the alliance. Part of the problem seems to stem from a feeling by ICI that Sumitomo negotiated an over-strong deal for themselves at the outset. This emphasizes the need to ensure that both sides benefit equally, since if they do not, negative attitudes will surely develop on the side of the partner that perceives itself to be the 'loser'. A senior ICI executive outlines the problem at ICI Pharma:

> We started with a 50/50 joint venture, and moved later to 60/40. We charged the JV with certain specific tasks; mainly marketing and sales. Sumitomo did the manufacturing, i.e. making the tablets and the distribution, and also the registration. But over time we have been trying to take back the manufacturing as we felt they were getting an unfair profit from this. . . . The stresses and strains in the relationship mainly stem, I think, from the fact that we've come to believe that the deal we gave Sumitomo for the manufacturing was over the odds. But it has been hard to renegotiate.

However, it would seem to be not just an over-strong deal negotiated by Sumitomo that has made attitudes less than optimal; there seems also to be, at least by ICI, a fundamental difficulty in moving mentally out of the strong ICI culture into a sensitive understanding of partners from other cultures. The ICI Pharma joint venture has been in existence since 1972, yet a senior ICI executive can still say:

> One of the things that still holds us back in Japan is our lack of understanding of Japanese culture. Relationships are very important in Japan, and we are much less certain about what might spoil a relationship than we would be with a European or US company.

In the Courtaulds/Nippon Paint alliance, attitude problems also seem to have placed a brake on the development of the relationship. As Derek Welch, the Courtaulds 'gateway', says, the alliance started off well because the people setting it up were sensitive to their cultural differences:

> then there were people changes, and the older people who knew Nippon very well retired, and the younger people came in and didn't understand the Japanese culture, and way of doing things. They saw them as a licensee, and treated them as such. Nippon were very polite, and didn't tell us, until about 8 months ago when a new man took over at their end who had worked in the US and he told us a few home truths. We then realized that things were coming unstuck on marine, and the territorial issue was just a symptom. . . . We investigated and found that in Courtaulds there was a fair amount of NIH around, and we weren't giving them a fair crack of the whip. . . . But to do what he did that day he had to act against Japanese culture. He also stopped some NIH at their end. . . . Most Japanese will go out of their way not to upset us, so they may not always tell us the truth. It is difficult to convince them that we want to know the truth, not hear things that will not upset us. Normally you will only find out what they really think if you employ a Japanese, then they may talk Japanese to Japanese.

This passage demonstrates the inherent difficulties involved in adopting and maintaining positive co-operative attitudes in international strategic alliances. The differences between the questionnaire responses and the detailed interview 'story telling' also shows the degree to which company personnel feel the need to claim that their company has good sensitive attitudes, even in the face of related incidents that cast some doubt on this. This internal conflict only emphasizes the apparent importance of the attitude question in sustaining a positive alliance relationship. Honesty is vital not just with one's partner but also with oneself, in order to achieve a real assessment of the situation. In some of the alliances investigated, notably Rover/Honda, C&W, RBS/Santander and ICL/Fujitsu, this self-critical aspect seems to have achieved and to have retained prominence to the ensuing benefit of the alliance.

As Professor Teramoto emphasized (Teramoto *et al.*, 1991):

The presence of complementarity of resources and closeness is a necessary condition for different organizations to create a new value system together, which would enable them to set clear common strategic objectives. Clear objectives require an effective coordination between companies, which includes successful reciprocity. In this way organizations concerned can learn from one another in the process of allying. In other words, an inter-firm link is a dynamic process which expands intraorganizational learning into producing much greater results.

The statistical picture of partner attitudes

In the statistical analysis of the 67 alliances, partner attitudes was shown to be the area most significantly and importantly associated with alliance effectiveness. Figure 7.1 shows the comparative level of the various management factors re-vealed as important in relation to alliance success.

'Top management commitment' recorded very strong significance scores when correlated with alliance success. For details, see the statistics in Appendix B. It is important to stress that the consensus of the respondents from 67 alliances implies that if top management is highly committed to an alliance it will probably prove to be effective, and if top management is not so committed, the alliance is likely to fail. No variables related to strategic fit, for example, showed values anywhere near as high. Lower level commitment is also regarded as very important.

'Mutual trust' scores almost as highly as 'top management commitment'. There is obviously a strong relationship between these two variables in most circumstances, since, although they describe different aspects of positive partner attitudes, it is difficult to imagine high top management commitment being associated with mutual mistrust. This is nevertheless possible in circumstances where, for example, the alliance is seen as crucial to the firm's survival, but the behaviour of the partner is suspected of being solely self-interested.

Sensitivity to the partner's culture is also seen as very closely associated with alliance success. This factor, perhaps

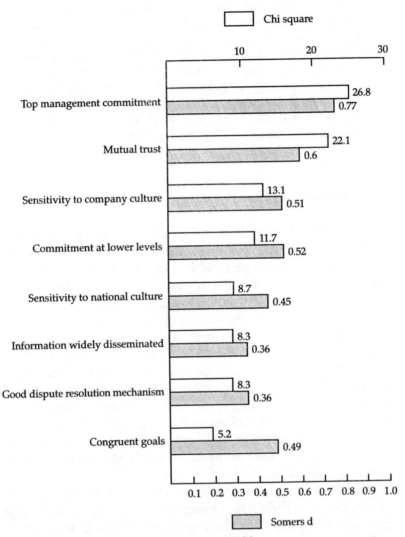

Figure 7.1 The significant management variables

not surprisingly, is seen as more important than sensitivity to the partner's national culture, which is however still a significant factor. The two factors are shown in the cluster analysis to be strongly mutually dependent.

The dominant importance of the inter-personal aspects of alliances then emerges very strongly from both the in-depth ten-case analysis and the statistical 67-case analysis. Respondents found more difficulty in relating underlying cost and strategic factors to alliance effectiveness. This does not refute the possible importance of the economic forces, but it does consign them to a subliminal, largely unperceived, role.

SUMMARY

This chapter has described the conclusions that emerged from the case studies and the statistical analysis in relation to the management factors that matter if an alliance is to be successful. In summary, positive partner attitudes has emerged on all counts as the most important factor associated with alliance effectiveness. The attitudes reflected in sensitivity to culture, mutual trust and strong commitment have been seen to be of paramount importance. Organizational arrangements, especially with regard to boundary-spanning activity, have also been highlighted as very important. The question of congruent objectives, however, remains shrouded in ambiguity. Questionnaire respondents in the case studies and in the overall statistical analysis overwhelmingly claim that their objectives do not conflict with those of their partners, thereby disqualifying it as a discriminating factor associated with varying levels of alliance effectiveness. However, the case study transcripts tell a different story, and suggest that the changing nature of underlying corporate objectives plays an important role in determining the effectiveness of the alliances.

8 EVC: a joint venture between ICI and Enichem

This case study and the next illustrate, both positively and negatively, the management factors important for alliance effectiveness.

In the fourth quarter of 1984, ICI began discussions with Enichem of Italy with a view to setting up a manufacturing and marketing joint venture to provide leadership in the rationalization of the ageing vinylchloride and polyvinyl chloride (PVC) market in Europe, which was plagued with excess capacity. ICI had already started the process by acquiring the PVC interests of BP and Lonrho. Similarly, Enichem, with the same purpose in mind, represented a consortium of the PVC interests of the Italian companies ANIC, Pozzi, Rumianca, SIR, Montedison and Liquichimica. After a long drawn-out negotiation between the companies and with the European Commission, the joint venture was set up and began trading as EVC, i.e. European Vinyls Corporation, on 1 October 1986.

THE MARKET

Until the early 1980s the European commodity plastics market was regional, with few imports from outside the region. Western Europe had a demand level of about 4 million tonnes, North America had about 3.25 million tonnes, and SE Asia was growing fast with 1 million tonnes in Japan and 1.5 million tonnes elsewhere in the region. The Asian demand in excess of their production capacity was imported from North America and Europe at that time. In 1982 there was about 1 million tonnes of excess capacity in Europe, much of which was exported to the Far East.

The 1970s had caused underlying structural changes in the level of demand for bulk chemicals that worked their way through in the early 1980s. The oil price shocks of 1973 and 1978 had led to a dramatic reduction in demand for oil-based products by 1982. This was compounded by the onset of recession, and demand for PVC fell 20 per cent in that year. There was also the fact that PVC had become a low-cost throw-away material, and faced a largely saturated market in western Europe; the growth for PVC was forecast to be negligible in the foreseeable future; and efforts to increase the recycling characteristics of PVC reduced the demand for new product.

In the meantime, ICI had built a new PVC plant at Wilhelmshafen in Germany, with a capacity for 120 000 tonnes. This came on stream just when demand was very low, giving ICI a lot of surplus capacity. Enichem had been formed by the Italian government from six Italian chemical companies, all of which were technically bankrupt. In 1983 there were 4 million tonnes of demand in Europe and 5 million tonnes of capacity, and the UK and Italy had the largest surpluses of supply over demand.

As the 1980s progressed, the market changed from being basically regional to clearly global, mainly owing to the growth of the Far East producers. Shintec Shinetsu of Japan and Formosa Plastics of Taiwan both established manufacturing bases in the USA, and are now the biggest producers

Table 8.1 *The European plastics market*

	1992 capacity (tonnes)	Market share (%)
EVC	1 200 000	20
Solvay	1 000 000	17
ATO	680 000	12
Rovin/Shell	485 000	8
LVM	390 000	7
HULS	380 000	7
Wacker	360 000	6
Norsk	355 000	6

in the USA and in the world. It is believed in the industry that within the next five years they will probably establish bases in Europe also. They are already major exporters into the region. In 1986 this was not foreseen by either ICI or Enichem, and did not feature in their strategic planning.

In 1992, however, EVC was the largest western European commodity plastics company, as shown in Table 8.1.

MANAGEMENT

The creation of a joint venture between ICI and Enichem to attack the problem of excess capacity in the plastics industry was the appropriate approach. However the detailed arrangements were not so appropriate. A distinct company able to deal at arm's length with the shareholders was not created. The key production assets remained in the shareholder companies and the chief executive of the joint venture had only limited authority over some of the key staff. Prices of raw materials were decided by the shareholder suppliers, and Chief executive was permitted to go to the market for only 10 per cent of his raw material needs.

The combined capacity of Enichem and ICI was 1.5 million tonnes of vinylchloride and 1.25 million tonnes of polyvinylchloride, and it was judged that about 25 per cent of this, i.e. 300 000 tonnes of capacity, had to be withdrawn. ICI and Enichem conducted an enquiry in 1985 to determine the plants that should be withdrawn, as it was realized that the decisions might not affect the partners equally. The aim was to withdraw capacity without losing sales, and hence reduce the losses the two companies were suffering. Partly for this reason, it was decided to retain ownership of the assets concerned in the partner companies, and rent them as appropriate to EVC.

The management systems and attitudes in the alliance were only moderately successful. The shareholders gave only limited authority to the venture management team to run their own business in the way they knew best. Consequently, the chief executive needed highly developed political skills.

In fact John York comments as follows, when suggesting rules to guide joint venture chief executives:

> Recognize that the shareholders will tend to be economical with the truth on occasions opposite each other and opposite joint venture management. Accept that sometimes each shareholder will put his own interests ahead of the joint venture's interests. Accept that an equivalent measure of discontent from each shareholder is generally a measure of the even-handedness of joint venture management.

This suggests a less than smooth operation of management between shareholders and joint venture staff. It would seem that on systems and attitudes there was less than complete harmony. Furthermore, as became apparent, the longer term goals of the partners were somewhat divergent. PVC was very important to Enichem, but rather less so to ICI. The partners' interests coincided only in both being concerned to reduce the level of over-capacity in the industry in an orderly fashion.

The two companies exhibited interesting cultural differences in how they arrived at decisions. ICI held structured meetings from which decisions emerged but found them difficult to implement as people tended to work behind the scenes to subvert decisions with which they did not agree. Enichem were very functionally driven, and did not like meetings. Functional experts within Enichem, however, easily implemented decisions after considerable informal discussion. After a period of time an EVC culture evolved from these contrasting styles that worked for EVC but made both sets of shareholders uncomfortable, since it clashed with their respective cultures.

From the start of the joint venture in 1986, there was an agreed three-year plan, which involved stemming the losses in the first two years, largely by capacity withdrawal and rationalization, with a move into profits in Year 3. At the end of the three years it was planned that the shareholders should be presented with a profitable company into which the shareholders could transfer the assets, or possibly wind-up or sell, depending on the joint venture company's performance and prospects. As it transpired, there was strong demand for PVC in the years 1986–89 and profit targets were achieved by the end of the first year, but in 1993 the ensuing deep recession had pushed the company back into losses.

PVC is used across the industrial spectrum, and particularly in the construction and packaging industries—areas hard hit by the recession. It is also considered that plant utilization rates need to be above 90 per cent of capacity to allow reasonable rates of return on investment to be achieved. This was possible for EVC up to 1990, but not subsequently.

It became apparent that ICI's long-term objectives were different from those of Enichem. For ICI the production of plastics was not a core business and its main concern was to retrieve the business from a loss-making situation. It was not interested in expansion, however, if it meant more investment. For Enichem, the area did represent part of its core business, as it was in fact the Italian chemical industry. As John York, stated:

> Culturally the way to get permission to close down an old plant in Italy is to promise to build a new one in exchange. But ICI were more interested in areas that economize on capital investment.

The balance of production, and sales to EVC, was also different between the partners. Enichem are the largest producer of polyethylene in western Europe with over 1 million tonnes of capacity. EVC buys ethylene equally from ICI and Enichem, but this represents more than half of ICI's total production but only 20 per cent of Enichem's; however, the reverse applies in chloride, where ICI is the bigger producer.

While the capacity withdrawal plan was being put into operation, EVC acquired BICC's compounding businesses in the UK, and also bought an Italian compounding company. The acquisitions were financed out of retained profits, and EVC now had an area in which it owned its assets. A further acquisition was an industrial film-fabricating company in Italy, which had synergies with ICI's German film-fabricating company which EVC had also purchased. The companies manufactured film for industrial and pharmaceutical purposes.

EVC grew rapidly from an initial £500 million business to one of about £1 billion. As it did not own its plants, the level of central staff was fairly small, and during the period did not exceed 100, of whom about 40 were seconded from the shareholder companies, with the remainder being recruited locally. ICI tended to provide marketing secondees and Enichem production staff. The secondees had 'return tickets' to their parent companies and remained on their original pension schemes.

The problems caused by the shareholders' decision to retain the production plants on their own balance sheets meant that EVC had to operate them under lease. They were still manned by ICI and Enichem staff, which made control of operational efficiencies difficult as the EVC chief executive had no real line authority over the production personnel. The plants were sited on ICI or Enichem estates, and EVC had no real control over their operation. As John York stated:

> We can control the secondees in Brussels, and the local hires. We control the selling operations in the field. All the compounding and fabrication staff are ours now, so of the 6000 people employed two-thirds are now ours; we pay their salaries. But some of the most important guys aren't, e.g. the production operators on the key sites.

Also EVC had to accept raw material prices set by the shareholder suppliers. These were above the market price level and included shareholder level overheads, which were high. If EVC could have bought its raw materials from a third party, it could have obtained much lower prices.

Once the company became profitable in 1988, the shareholders believed that the problem that EVC was set up to solve was solved. They did not appreciate the vulnerability of a commodity plastics company of the size of EVC to fluctuations in industrial activity, and thus the shareholder euphoria of 1988 gave way to depression in 1992 as profits reversed into losses. In 1990 there were rumours of a possible sale of EVC to Occidental Petroleum, America's largest domestic PVC producers, but the sale did not happen.

In July 1992, in concert with its major competitors Solvay, Atochem and Huls, EVC was investigated by the European Commission for possible cartel creation. This followed a similar investigation four years previously, which led to large fines that were subsequently annulled by the European Court of First Instance on technical grounds. Clearly, whether a cartel was operating or not, the major European PVC producers were finding it difficult to make a profit during the recession, and in competition with the Far East. Prices had slumped from DM 1.75 to DM 1.00 per tonne during 1991, and it was estimated that they would need to be at least DM 1.45 if the companies were to break even. Facing this, the industry attempted to achieve a price increase of 30 per cent, but in the face of falling demand failed to achieve this, and stimulated the cartel investigation.

The joint venture is not characterized as one in which organizational learning became a key aspect, with consequent intangible benefits to the shareholders in areas that might not have been anticipated. John York comments again:

> I don't believe the shareholders have learned much from the venture, which is a pity, as next time they will have to start all over again.

SUMMARY

The joint venture has to be regarded as relatively successful, since it achieved its primary objective of returning the area to profit in normal non-recessionary times largely through rationalization of capacity and improvements in efficiency. Owing to the limited appreciation by the shareholders of the most appropriate principles to follow if a joint venture company is to be well managed and to thrive over time, and to the somewhat bleak prospects for PVC in the medium-term future, a prognosis for the longer term future would need to be more cautious, given current shareholder systems and attitudes. Perhaps the best solution for all the partners would be a third party sale, as was apparently in prospect in 1990. In fact in November 1992 Hoechst announced a merger of its PVC interests with those of Wacker, which was heralded in the press as probably the first of the next phase of industry rationalization. EVC cannot realistically participate in this process until it has ownership of its manufacturing and, possibly, raw material-producing plants, so that the joint venture can present itself as a self-supporting business.

The fact that EVC was forced to buy 90 per cent of its raw materials at above market prices from the shareholders, and that production took place in factories owned by the partners and not by EVC, considerably constrained its developmental potential.

9 Courtaulds Coatings and Nippon Paint

The collaboration alliance between Courtaulds Coatings and Nippon Paint of Japan was formed in 1976. It covers marine coatings in the areas of marketing and sales, research and development, and the exchange of technology. Courtaulds have integrated Nippon into what they describe as their marine worldwide commercial network. Through the alliance, Courtaulds have established an effective presence in Japan, and Nippon have been assisted in rising from No. 4 in the Japanese marine paint market to No. 2.

THE WORLD PAINT INDUSTRY

The world paint industry has been restructured over the last decade by a number of major mergers, acquisitions and disposals; notably in 1985 and 1986, ICI bought Glidden in the USA for £300 million, and BASF bought Inmont for $1 billion, turning both acquirers into global paints and coatings companies. The global leaders in the paint industry in 1991, ranked by sales in million litres, are shown in Table 9.1.

The paint industry can be divided into two main product classes:

1. Architectural paints for the decoration of buildings and homes. These are high volume and low priced.
2. Industrial coatings which impart properties and add value to industrial goods. They are higher priced and form a vast array of niche markets across the globe.

Table 9.1 *The world paint industry*

Company	Sales (litres x10⁶)	Company	Sales (litres x10⁶)
AKZO-Nobel (NF)	840	**Nippon (Japan)**	**350**
ICI (UK)	805	**Courtaulds (UK)**	**300**
Sherwin-Williams (US)	533	Kansai (Japan)	280
PPG (US)	515	DuPont (US)	265
BASF (Germany)	500	Valspar (US)	200

Source: ICI

Courtaulds and PPG of the USA, the world's fourth largest paint company, have managed their growth with less risky strategies than those, such as ICI, involved in the acquisitions of unfamiliar companies. PPG has grown more organically in a global sense by acquiring its licensees, and has largely confined itself to the automotive market. Courtaulds has opted to attempt to strengthen its position in the world market for marine paint, which was becoming less attractive to others due to the long-term decline in the number of ships, and also in other markets where global strengths are a key to growth, such as the new powder coatings and car coatings markets. However, Courtaulds still has more than one-third of world sales in this market. PPG and Courtaulds also seem to have reduced any future threat from Japan by developing alliances with Nippon Paint— PPG in automotive coatings and Courtaulds in marine paints. Kansai, the other Japanese major paint company, is aggressively looking westward, and has developed an alliance with DuPont. The other major paint companies have a strong regional bias. For example, the world's No. 3, Sherwin-Williams, has more than 90 per cent of its volume in the USA.

The paint market is an attractive one if managed properly. Conway Ivy, treasurer of Sherwin-Williams says: 'This business isn't recession-proof, but it's certainly recession resistant.' (*Financial Times*, 27 March 1991). John Danzeisen, financial controller of ICI Paints, adds:

'We are not a star like pharmaceuticals, but we are a lot safer and lower risk. Why be in paint? Because there are always returns in good times or bad times. I cannot think of a day when we have lost money, nor can I contemplate such a thing.' (*Financial Times,* 27 March 1991)

In marine paints a ban was issued in Japan in 1992 on tin-based anti-fouling paints, i.e. those containing tributyl tin compounds, known as TBT. Since the ban only applies in Japan, and tin-free paints cost twice as much as tin-based ones and do not provide a comparable performance, this ban is affecting Japanese shipyards negatively as dry-docking work goes to restriction-free Singapore and Korea.

Kansai are showing aggressive international leanings in the marine area, and most other leading Japanese companies have formed European alliances. The Hyundai subsidiary, Korean Chemical Company (KCC), is also showing great interest in markets outside South-East Asia and has signed a number of international licences, e.g. with ICI, Berger and Ameron Marine Coatings Division. ICI are now in three markets—architectural, car coatings and the automotive after-market.

KCC has the largest dedicated paint factory in the world. It was established in 1974 to service shipbuilding requirements, but these now account for only 10 per cent of KCC's current turnover, as the company has diversified extensively into other paint market areas.

COURTAULDS COATINGS

Within Courtaulds plc, with over £2 billion sales and £200 million pre-tax profit in 1992–93, Coatings accounts for 35 per cent of the sales and 27 per cent of the profits. The breakdown by product division is as shown in Table 9.2.

Courtaulds Coatings' strategy involves developing a strong international position in specialist markets that are technically demanding and require high levels of service. Its key product areas are marine coatings, protective coatings, powder coatings and aerospace coatings, architectural paints

Table 9.2 *Courtaulds plc*

Sales		Profits
35%	Coatings	27%
10%	Performance materials	8%
13%	Packaging	13%
10%	Chemicals	19%
23%	Fibres and films	33%

in the US and Australasia, and packaging and coil coatings in Europe, Brazil and Asia-Pacific.

Despite current recessionary conditions in most coatings markets, marine coatings were buoyant, especially in the Far East with a successful introduction of tin-free anti-fouling paints. Sales in the yacht market, however, were more sluggish. Courtaulds marine coatings are led by the world's most popular brand 'International', which is backed by a global distribution service of over 500 locations. Customers are guaranteed a comprehensive and consistent product range throughout the world. At Courtaulds, R&D activity is the highest in the world in marine paints, and the company is acknowledged as a major innovator in the industry. Courtaulds, as world leader in marine paints, have a market share more than double their nearest rival. They have 40 per cent of the market for ships over 4000 tonnes dead weight, and for the market overall they command between 25 and 30 per cent.

NIPPON PAINT

Although Nippon Paint appears higher on the world ranking of paint companies than does Courtaulds Coatings, this is largely attributable to its strong position in automotive paints. In marine paints, the area to which the alliance is related, Nippon Paint is much smaller than Courtaulds Coatings.

In the initial stages of the alliance, Nippon Paint were No. 4 in the Japanese marine paint market. However, they have succeeded in improving this position over time, and are now a very strong No. 2, behind the Japanese market leader Chugoku. Their R&D position is also strong, and they are quite capable of developing innovative new products on their own. In fact Derek Welch the Courtaulds general manager with responsibility for the relationship, regards the present partnership as technically equal.

Although Nippon were content with a national position at the start of the agreement, they are now increasingly ambitious internationally. From the Nippon viewpoint, Hiroshi Takahashi, a Nippon divisional director, claims that Nippon's objective has always been to develop its business in marine paint globally. He also states:

> Nippon has superior technology for new buildings paint over Courtaulds. Courtaulds are best on paint for repairs, and have very strong global marketing power.

The alliance was set up as a collaboration because no specific business arrangements were prescribed. Courtaulds were to provide product and technology, as were Nippon reciprocally. Nippon was to act as Courtaulds' Japanese agents, and to exercise non-competitive restraint in territories outside Japan. As Takahashi states:

> The merchandising power and technological development power of both partners is strong. Nippon is superior in technological development in some products and Courtaulds has very strong global marketing power, which means we have a synergy effect. The strengths of the partners are complementary, not competing. This was not the case at the beginning, but it is now.

Prior to the alliance with Nippon, Courtaulds had attempted, unsuccessfully, to enter the Japanese market. It also attempted a joint venture with Chugoku, the Japanese market leader, but this failed because of Chugoku's international ambitions. The agreement with Nippon, which was based on the understanding that Nippon had no such ambitions, had three basic objectives:

1.   To co-operate in the technological area of marine coatings.
2.   To establish a working relationship so that Nippon would represent Courtaulds and service its international customers in Japan, and Courtaulds would service Nippon's customers outside Japan.
3.   To market a dual product range in Japan, which meant taking the best of both companies' products and selling them on one price list containing the names of both companies.

Once the deal was struck, the new partners had immediately to unravel any conflicting arrangements they had with other parties. This was quite complicated, as Courtaulds had to retrench from their existing Japanese arrangements, and Nippon were involved in various network arrangements, in traditional Japanese fashion. It was agreed that Nippon would not compete in areas of the world where Courtaulds was represented, which meant most of the world outside Japan. However, there were a number of 'free' territories, e.g. China, Vietnam, Cambodia, and Taiwan. It was agreed that if either company made sales in those territories, it would pay the other a commission. If either company wished to set up a joint venture in any of these countries, it had to split its shareholding with the other.

MANAGEMENT

The 'gateway' principle operates in the alliance, whereby one person is responsible for all contacts to Courtaulds. When this system was relaxed in the late 1980s, relationships began to founder. At the Japanese end there is some confusion, since Nippon has an International Division and a Marine Division and internal tensions can occur between them.

Overall attitudes, commitment and trust are generally good, which has enabled the partners to overcome any problems that might emerge from internal politics, possible conflicting long-term objectives, or cultural dissimilarities. Ultimately, however, the non-competitive agreement that restricts Nippon marine paints from entering the world outside Japan must prove increasingly difficult to accept as Nippon's growing success and strength widens its corporate objectives and ambitions.

Different cultures have proved somewhat problematical in the relationship. Courtaulds were reluctant to divulge more technical information than they considered necessary. The Japanese were eager to discover any information they could. Technologically, Nippon wanted to be regarded as an equal, but met with a certain patronising attitude in Courtaulds, receiving the famous 'Not Invented Here' syndrome from Courtaulds' technologists. Also, the Japanese are very thorough, and will not launch a product until they are absolutely sure it is right. In the West more risks are taken with product launches, and the Mark 2 product tends to be much better than the Mark 1. Takahashi believes that Nippon and Courtaulds have different attitudes to strategic development and risk.

> We should be clearer about our respective globalization policies. Courtaulds are more risk taking than we are. They go where there is demand. This is their action principle. This can lead to misunderstanding as we are more cautious.

These cultural differences required adjustment on both sides, and the problems did not become apparent until the dynamism started to go out of the alliance with the achievement of the initial objectives.

The alliance displayed three distinct phases, which are summarized here but explained in more detail below.

1. The first phase ran from 1976 to the mid-1980s. During this phase the initial objectives were substantially realized.
2. The second phase was one of stagnation and frustration, particularly for Nippon, as the restrictive aspects of the alliance were realized as they gained strength in the marine market.
3. In the third phase strong attempts were made to create further development in the relationship, through a

much closer and real R&D cooperation in marine, and more particularly through the coil-coating joint venture set up to market into continental Europe.

1. At the outset of the alliance, it took about two years to effect the transition from existing relationships, and then to agree product ranges. The alliance then got into high gear with Courtaulds' new self-polishing polymer, which was an improved anti-fouling agent and saved on fuel consumption. It was branded 'Intersmooth'. The alliance thus had a good start with the innovative 'Intersmooth' range, and with the improved service in Japan that Nippon was able to give Courtaulds' customers. This carried matters through the 1970s and the early 1980s.

2. The alliance then began to stagnate, since both parties had achieved their initial objectives. Nippon had climbed to No. 2 in Japan, and Courtaulds had an impressive Japanese servicing agent. At this point Nippon became more interested in developing outside Japan, but Courtaulds already had a fairly comprehensive world network, so objectives began to conflict. There were also problems in the free territories. Courtaulds proposed to set up a joint venture in China, and although Nippon had always been informed and had declined to participate, they suddenly demanded to participate at the last moment when the negotiations were complete. This was not possible, and caused some friction, Courtaulds believing that Nippon's actions were intended to create a lever to persuade Courtaulds to agree to Nippon's operation outside Japan.

3. A more positive development has occurred in coil coating where, as mentioned above, Nippon has set up a joint venture with Courtaulds to launch coil-coating products into Europe. The joint venture has access to both Nippon and Courtaulds technology, thus guaranteeing a very good product range. It also gives Courtaulds access to Japanese methods of production management and Nippon's customer service concept, to stimulate organizational learning. This new endeavour has rejuvenated the alliance after its period of stagnation.

Whether the alliance will provide a permanent or only a

temporary phase of Courtaulds Coatings and Nippon's development into clearly global companies will depend on the reactions of both partners to the partially restrictive agreements.

SUMMARY

The alliance has a mixture of good and limiting characteristics. On the good side, both partners have benefited substantially from the relationship, and show characteristics of trust, commitment and increasing sensitivity to cultural differences. However, overall objectives increasingly cease to be congruent as Nippon becomes more successful and develops global ambitions. There is also little evidence of bonding, or of organizational learning, although, after a period of stagnation, this is currently taking place to some degree. The alliance has endured for a long time, and its prospects for the future probably depend crucially on the level of bonding achieved by the new generation of senior executives in both companies, and on the partners' ability to reconcile their objectives and achieve greater organizational learning. There is little doubt that both partners value the relationship greatly, although their respective objectives and views of each other differ to some degree. To Nippon, Courtaulds is a very strong global marketing company with whom it is happy to share joint global development. However, Nippon considers that it is stronger technologically. Courtaulds also see Nippon as greatly improved technologically, and as a strong partner to represent them in Japan, but probably not as an equal global partner in the worldwide marine paints market.

10 The evolving alliance: a limited, latent or dynamic relationship?

Alliances that remain in existence will always have their claimants to success. Similarly, those that are dissolved will frequently be classed as failures. Yet such a simple classification is rarely appropriate. An existing alliance may have lost its way and been marginalized in the partners' priorities, yet lacked anyone with the interest to dissolve it. Correspondingly, owing to revised strategic imperatives or significant environmental change, an effective alliance may no longer meet the future needs of the partners and be dissolved. The effectiveness of alliances needs to be assessed in a rather less simplistic fashion. This chapter considers the nature of an alliance's evolution and its relationship to its ultimate effectiveness. It also considers the whole question of effectiveness in alliances. What is it, and where are the keys to achieving it?

In this book an effective alliance has been defined as one that:

(a) is achieving measurable and predefined objectives
(b) may have achieved other spin-off benefits
(c) exhibits high morale within the alliance
(d) has developed a good reputation in the partner companies
(e) has a good reputation in the industry.

The definition of effectiveness can be normative—'the alliance is effective if both partners feel it is'—or descriptive, if appropriate yardsticks can be identified to measure effectiveness. An attempt has been made to establish such yardsticks in criteria (a) and (b) above. Criteria (c), (d) and (e) refer to more subjective evaluations—so-called 'feel good' factors.

ALLIANCE CLASSIFICATION

In the process of developing the case studies, it became clear that it is possible to classify surviving alliances into three levels of effectiveness: limited, latent and dynamic.

Limited alliances

These alliances seem to be of limited future potential for a number of reasons. They include EVC, ICI Pharma, and Imperial/Wintermans. EVC has been set up to rationalize the European PVC market. Its probable future may be total acquisition by Enichem, or by a third party, as the unattractiveness of the market makes natural evolution difficult. ICI Pharma is shrinking in importance as ICI and Sumitomo pursue development through other vehicles. Imperial/Wintermans may have developed as far as it can develop. Wintermans' owners, BAT, are strong competitors of Imperial, and are becoming more closely involved in the management of Wintermans. Also, the original objectives of the alliance have been achieved, and the partners' objectives no longer seem congruent. The key factor in limited alliances is that, given their history and current situation, they no longer seem to have the potential for further evolution.

Latent alliances

These alliances have been effective by many measures, but have at least one constraining factor that prevents them from wholly realizing their potential. This category includes Dowty–Sema, Eurobrek, the Cable and Wireless consortium and Courtaulds/Nippon Paint. Dowty–Sema wins government contracts, but it does not make profit on them, and its cultural sensitivities and organizational arrangements do not encourage efficient operation. Eurobrek is a young alliance, but its lack of obvious competitive advantage *vis-à-vis* Kelloggs, and its organizational rigidity in not allowing the venture to control its own salesforce, suggests an inflexibility that may impede its growth into the dynamic category. However, UKCO and USCO are powerful partners and a dynamic future may well lie ahead, given more flexible attitudes. The Cable and Wireless consortium has been successful in a very challenging market, but is still not profitable. Also, its future is thought to be uncertain as the partners all have differing agendas. The Courtaulds/Nippon Paint alliance has had problems for reasons of cultural misunderstanding and conflict of objectives, but these factors are now understood and it could easily gain a new dynamism if they are solved successfully. The key difference between a dynamic and a latent alliance may well lie in one or more attitude, or constraining factor, that inhibits the latent alliance from realizing its full potential.

Dynamic alliances

These generally achieve their set objectives, and also perhaps unexpected side benefits. Morale is usually high in those involved in the alliance, and in the partner companies, and the reputations of both the alliance and the partner companies is respected in the industry. They seem to achieve together the sustainable competitive advantage that the partners cannot achieve as separate entities. In the qualitative research Rover/Honda, ICL/Fujitsu, and RBS/Santander clearly meet these criteria.

ALLIANCE EVOLUTION

Of the cases studied, the most effective alliances seem to be those that show positive evolution over time, rather than merely a competent pursuit of the objectives agreed at their formation. Achrol *et al.* (1990) describe the four stages of alliance development in their schema as entrepreneurship, collectivity and formalization leading to domain elaboration. Thus alliances are, they suggest, typically fluid and creative at the outset; and this stage is followed by one of collectivity where a defined sense of mission is developed. The formalization stage involves the development of systems and procedures, and ultimately the domain elaboration stage is one of self-renewal, described in this book as evolution, where flexibility should be renewed. Lorange and Roos (1992) stress that evolution is much more important to an alliance than control by its partners: 'Alliances should evolve, so excessive concern with controls can be counter-productive.'

A consideration of the propositions concerning alliance evolution may reveal some insights into why surviving alliances fall into each of the above three categories of limited (i.e. little potential for evolution), latent (i.e. could evolve if some energy releasing changes were made) or dynamic (i.e. evolving).

Alliances are normally set up for specific purposes. They may be focused on the synergies available from the fusion of key competencies from the partners directed towards a specific target, or the interaction may be more complex. If the initial purpose or relationship scope remains the only one, the alliance may be unlikely to enter the dynamic category. This is borne out by evidence from the case studies. Lorange and Probst (1987) emphasize that many alliances fail because they have not had sufficient adaptive properties built into them to cope with evolutionary pressures. Some redundant resources must, they believe, be committed to the alliances to achieve sufficient flexibility for development. The combating of entropy is seen by Thorelli (1986) as the key reason for pursuing the path of evolution, and a feeling that where there is no longer growth, the onset of decay may not be far away. Figure 10.1 shows the relative importance of the various significant evolution variables in relation to their strength of association with alliance success.

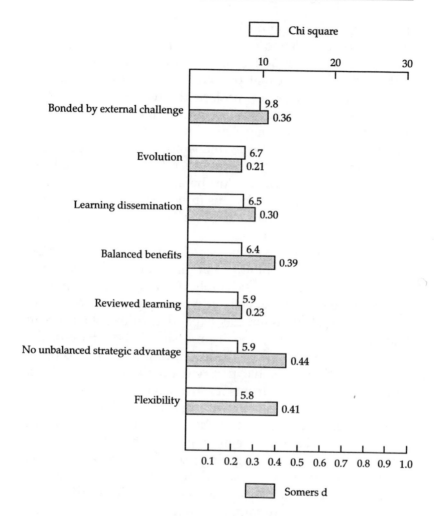

Figure 10.1   The significant evolution variables

New projects

The *limited* category of alliances shows little sign of evolution. EVC is a prime candidate for sale, having achieved its primary objectives of PVC sector rationalization. However, owing partly to the purchasing and production limitations placed on it by the partner companies, it has not managed to achieve a low enough cost base to become profitable during the downswing of the business cycle. To be saleable it will need to become endowed by the partners with its full complement of productive assets. ICI Pharma was set up with an arrangement that proved insufficiently attractive to entice ICI to put more new projects through the venture. As a result, the venture will continue during the life of its current product portfolio, but may have few prospects beyond that. Imperial Tobacco and Wintermans seem to have reached a natural limit to their co-operative endeavour, especially in view of Wintermans ownership by an arch competitor BAT, and the partners' lack of obvious future potential synergies.

In the statistical analysis the overall evolution variable was identified as very important.

The *latent* category alliances have shown substantial developments, but exhibit major limitations. Dowty–Sema has expanded very considerably from a 'shop window' beginning, and now has claims to be a substantial company in its own right. Its remit has expanded from submarine to include surface vessels; and from a single client base of the UK Ministry of Defence, it is now lifting its sights to other navies, e.g. Korea. Its 100 per cent purchase by Bae–Sema may well release it from its management systems and attitudes constraints; yet currently it is believed to make little if any profit, and is beset by inter-cultural problems. Eurobek, from its shell beginning, soon bought the RHM cereal interests in the UK, giving itself 14 per cent of the UK market as a result of the acquisition, and is proceeding to launch new brands at an energetic rate. If it can show genuine competitive advantage in relation to Kelloggs, it may become dynamic. Yet the staff display doubts about its long-term future, and the 'good' relationship between the partners seems more instrumental than emotional. C&W is using its consortium experience of working in the Japanese environ-ment to develop stronger networks for future projects, and the consortium itself is developing rapidly as a strong competitor to the ex-monopolist KDD. But the future objectives of the partners, and C&W's role in their plans, is far from certain. Courtaulds and Nippon Paint—after a period in which the alliance ceased to evolve as it had achieved its initial objectives—is now pursuing the development of new projects with a coil-coating joint venture into continental Europe and closer R&D co-operation. However, mutual understanding needs to be reinforced after a difficult period and the realization by Courtaulds that Nippon is now becoming a world-class organization.

The *dynamic* alliances—Rover/Honda, ICL/Fujitsu, and RBS/Santander—show a flow of new projects, additional area of co-operation and flexible adjustment to change. Rover/Honda began as an arm's-length imported knock-down kits arrangement between the companies, and has developed into a complex alliance covering most functions except sales and marketing, and with a 20 per cent share exchange. A technical support alliance between ICL and Fujitsu in 1981 has led to a far-ranging technology, product and marketing alliance, also with a large share interest of Fujitsu in ICL. The RBS/Santander alliance has expanded into a number of joint ventures and a consortium EEIG company to run the multi-partner multinational IBOS system. There has been share exchange commitment in all three cases.

Flexible adjustment

Flexibility in the relationship is obviously an important success factor, since it implies that when circumstances change, the alliance is allowed to reflect this in a sensitive way. It is interesting to consider the case studies to see how flexible in attitude they seem to be.

All of the dynamic alliances have shown considerable flexibility during their existence. Rover/Honda has been through five separate waves of activity, all placing different stresses and requirements on the staff, and has adjusted effectively to them. ICL/Fujitsu has had to cope with a changing relationship as Fujitsu moved into the position of a majority equity holder, and the alliance has had to suppress any possible risk to the relationship from that development and seems to have achieved this sensitively. RBS/Santander has adjusted to the setting up of several joint ventures in the relationship and the development of IBOS.

What of the latent alliances? Flexibility does not seem to have been totally absent here. C&W have certainly shown a very flexible attitude to getting established in Japan, even to the extent of contributing £17 million to the venture and not insisting on having cheque-signing authority. Dowty–Sema has also shown very flexible development, as its size has grown with increasing size of contract. Courtaulds/Nippon Paint have however, until recently, not been flexible enough to deal successfully with adjustments needed to their territorial agreement, and the Eurobrek venture also seems to be unduly rigid in its arrangements.

In the limited alliances, ICI Pharma has been somewhat inflexible not to have renegotiated the troublesome Sumitomo agreement. However, EVC has developed flexibly, as has Imperial/Wintermans. Overall, the relative importance of flexibility has been shown by its high rating in the statistical analysis.

Balanced development

The idea of balanced development suggests that, for the success of an alliance, one partner should not move strongly ahead of the other in the strategic and other benefits it receives from the partnership. However, this does not seem to be borne out very strongly by the evidence from the case studies. In the most dynamic category of alliances, performance and consequent relative strength varies considerably as might be expected, but this has not damaged the alliances. Notably, Honda is now a much larger and stronger company than Rover, and Rover, despite having gained enormously from the alliance, is probably still technologically dependent on Honda, as is conceded by John Bacchus, Rover's Director of Collaboration. Similarly, the ICL/Fujitsu alliance is very dynamic, yet clearly ICL is very dependent on Fujitsu for its future; in fact, the Japanese company now owns 80 per cent of the British company. Even in the most balanced dynamic alliance, RBS/Santander, the Spanish bank owns 10 per cent of RBS while RBS owns only 2.5 per cent of Santander.

However, in this instance an unbalanced strategic position does not seem to have developed.

Killing's (1983) research—showing that alliances in which one partner is dominant are often the most successful—may well be relevant here. This suggests that a dominant partner removes much of the ambiguity from a relationship, and introduces some of the advantages of hierarchy. Clarity of authority may then lead to improved performance as the inefficiencies of consensus building are replaced by clear leadership.

A further point that emerges—particularly in the alliances of Rover/Honda and ICL/Fujitsu—is that the partner benefiting less from the alliance does not tend to resent this as long as its benefits are still strongly positive. If one partner benefits at the expense of the other (Sumitomo over ICI Pharmaceutical) then resentment is more likely to develop to the detriment of the alliance.

Of the latent and limited categories, only ICI in relation to ICI Pharma reported unbalanced benefits to the partners, presumably reflecting their view that Sumitomo struck a deal at the outset that was clearly more profitable to the Japanese company than to ICI. It does not seem, therefore, that the condition of balanced benefits is problematic in alliance development, although, at the extreme, it may become a source of contention (e.g. AT&T and Olivetti) if other problems also arise. In the statistical analysis it does feature as significant, but not at a very high level.

Partner bonding

It is suggested by Thorelli (1986) that alliances that do not consciously evolve and create bonding mechanisms are affected by entropic forces, and gradually either cease to be important or even move towards dissolution. Three possible mechanisms have been identified as means whereby alliances may achieve effective bonding. Clearly, all three need not to be present in all alliances, and there may be other mechanisms; however, if no bonding mechanisms are present, the prognosis for the alliance may be poor, as the partners may be regarding it as a specific resource or skill substitution rather than an interactive collaboration.

The bonding mechanisms identified are:

1.   Resolving an external challenge together.
2.   Exchanging personnel at a number of levels on a regular basis.
3.   Developing a culture that is a combination of the partners' cultures.

Clearly, bonding will be easier to achieve in a joint venture company where the staff are working together, than in a collaboration where, typically, they are not. It may well be, as in EVC, that the joint venture develops a culture of its own which, to some degree, becomes in opposition to the culture of the shareholder partners. Also personnel exchange may be in the form of secondment to the joint venture, which will have a very different impact on the individual than a personnel exchange within the partner companies in collaborations. This idea is therefore probably best examined separately for joint ventures and non-joint ventures.

None of the joint ventures was classified in the dynamic category of alliances. The reason may be that they frequently only affect a limited part of the business of the partners. Collaborations may be more likely to affect all the partners, and consequently to have greater prominence in the partners' priorities. However, with the exception of ICI Pharma, the joint ventures found bonding both important and possible. All the joint ventures claimed to have faced an external challenge together, which is almost inevitable in the establishment of a new company. Those who experienced this process therefore developed close relationships. However, the boundary spanning bonding to the shareholder partners in the joint venture cases was not necessarily so close. John York of EVC even measured his unbiased success in running EVC partly by the degree to which both partners felt he was favouring the other. Dowty–Sema, Eurobrek and EVC executives each claimed to have developed a clear joint venture culture, although not in relation to the owning partners. On the other hand, ICI Pharma and the C&W consortium did not.

In the collaboration category, bonding was obviously a more difficult task, since the companies related at an overall corporate level, but still only a part of one partner's personnel had close exposure to the personnel of the other partner. Thus, Rover's manufacturing, design and technology staff have close relationships with Honda personnel, but sales and marketing staff do not. In these circumstances bonding strength varied considerably. It was high, and deliberately so in Rover/Honda and ICL/Fujitsu who claimed to have surmounted an external challenge successfully together, to exchange personnel regularly and to be in the process of developing a combined culture. Neither Imperial/Wintermans nor Courtaulds/Nippon Paint made any substantial claims to bonding in any of these areas. RBS/Santander claimed strong bonding through the external challenge and personnel exchange, but allowed the cultures of the Scottish and Spanish banks to remain different but bridgeable through mutual exposure and inter-personal sensitivity.

Of the limited category of alliances, all reported relatively poor bonding. ICI Pharma and Imperial/Wintermans made no claims to bonding with their partner, and while EVC bonded well in the joint venture, the relationships with the shareholders were less close.

This seems, therefore, to be an important issue for successful development, but presents different challenges for joint ventures and non-joint ventures. For joint ventures, bonding within the venture seems relatively straightforward, but the relationship between (a) the partner companies and (b) the partner companies and the joint venture, are more complex and difficult. In collaborations the challenge is to develop a mutually effective culture that spreads outwards, even to personnel not directly involved with alliance matters. In the absence of this, the cultural interface merely moves from that between the partner companies back into the partner companies themselves, where different cultures develop between those who are and those who are not actively involved in the alliances.

In the statistical analysis the importance of successfully surmounting an external challenge together rated highly as a circumstance likely to create bonding, and hence stimulate alliance effectiveness.

Organizational learning

The concept of the learning organization is currently much in prominence in academic and popular texts on management. Senge (1992) stresses that the dynamic enterprise of the future will build its competitive advantage on a number of disciplines, from personal mastery of skills to team learning, which are key factors in alliance development. In fact, in Senge's view (1990) the major leadership roles of the chief executive are:

(a)   to develop a vision
(a)   to establish a dynamic culture
(c)   to provide learning opportunities.

The changing role of learning is seen perhaps most contrastingly in the early days of the Rover/Honda relationship, where the then Rover chairman, Michael Edwardes, is reported to have regarded Honda as filling a gap in the Rover product line. In contrast, the current situation is that Rover has totally adopted the Honda philosophy of continuous learning and has even set up a company, The Rover Learning Business, to ensure that the philosophy becomes even more embedded in the organization.

In the case study interviews, the dynamic alliance companies lay great claim to placing organizational learning high on their list of priorities. Rover/Honda and ICL/Fujitsu have set up systems to disseminate information widely in the partner companies. RBS/Santander has not done this yet, but all three dynamic alliances regularly review what they have learned from the alliance and what they can learn next, which is the essence of the learning philosophy.

Of the latent group, only Courtaulds/Nippon Paint claim to have fully adopted the learning philosophy, although

C&W claim to make regular reviews of what they have learned from the alliance, as does Eurobrek. No effort seems to be made, however, to spread the learning to the wider organization. On the limited alliances—EVC, ICI Pharma and Imperial/Wintermans—none claims to have done any noticeable organizational learning.

The ease with which learning takes place within an alliance depends upon, first, the type of learning and, second, the relationship between the nature of the learning and the condition of the would-be receptor. Many alliances are formed for short-term gains or to deal with temporary situations. These obscure the nature of the true strategic alliance, in which the intent is a learning one—the enhancement of joint sustainable competitive advantage and the extension of individual and joint core competencies—and in which long-term mutual benefit is supported by trust, commitment and a willingness to be flexible and robust in dealing with the tensions inherent in the partnership.

The key learning dimensions of intent, receptivity, transferability and transparency, when associated with the different types of learning—namely, technology, process, opportunity, and the learning philosophy—lead to an extremely varied learning situation, alliance by alliance. Clearly, for the greatest benefit to be achieved by an alliance partner, the key learning dimensions need to be present in large measure. In all alliances, opportunity learning—e.g. who are the best distributors?—can be identified and achieved, and, with effort, technology learning also. These forms of learning can be most easily observed in the Imperial/Wintermans and ICI Pharma alliances. Process learning, and the highest form of all, the learning philosophy, take longer to achieve, and normally require a culture change before they are permanently embedded. These factors are most evident in the Rover/Honda and ICL/Fujitsu dynamic alliances, and to a growing extent in RBS/Santander. They are not the only reasons why these alliances are classed as dynamic, but are the ones that give the best expectation for future success. Continuous learning and flexibility to meet changing challenges may well be characteristics that are found together in dynamic alliances.

In the statistical analysis, 'organizational learning' rated highly as significantly associated with 'alliance effectiveness' and is confirmed to be a very important aspect of an effective alliance in both the qualitative and quantitative analyses.

THE CASE FINDINGS

The overall findings from the 10 case studies are illustrated in Figure 10.2.

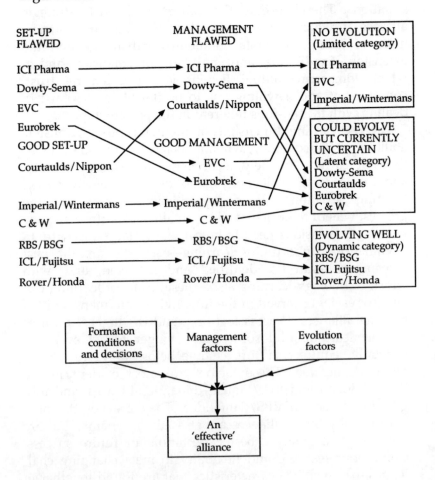

Figure 10.2 Findings from the qualitative research

An analysis of the limited alliances—namely, ICI Pharma, EVC and Imperial/Wintermans—also clearly showed where the problems lay in relation to the identified variables. ICI Pharma was formed in a way that at least ICI subsequently found unacceptable, as they believed that the alliance gave Sumitomo an excessively good deal at their expense. Subsequently, managerial attitudes were not positive and the alliance did not evolve. Thus, although some quantitative objective value was created, the alliance success was limited. EVC was set up in a limited form, with the joint venture having little control over its raw material supply or its production assets, and it operates in a market that is over-supplied. Thus, although it is well managed, and the joint venture personnel have developed positive attitudes, the alliance is thought unlikely to evolve, and divestment by one or both of the partners may be its fate. Imperial/Wintermans, although well organized and well managed, is likely to remain a limited alliance because of the ultimately conflicting objectives of the partners.

The latent category contains alliances that may well develop into more successful co-operative relationships, but are currently restricted by one factor or another. Dowty–Sema is very successful at obtaining orders and has shown dramatic expansion since its inception. However, it was set up as a 'shop window' company without its own assets, and seems to have been managed by committee, to the detriment of profits.

However, it has ultimately been acquired by Bae–Sema and may well thrive if its internal problems and differing agendas are resolved. The C&W consortium was well set up, and is well run. It is only in the latent category because the differing agendas of the shareholder partners make its longer term future uncertain. Eurobrek has to be regarded as latent for a number of reasons. It has only been in existence since 1989 and must be uncertain whether or not it has sustainable competitive advantage in the breakfast cereals market in relation to the market leader Kelloggs; if not, this must affect the long-term attitudes of its owners, USCO and UKCO. It has currently a further weakness: although it is a distinct business, the partners have not endowed it with a comprehensive self-sustaining set of assets. UKCO still does its selling and this dependency may well prove a limitation on ultimate success.

The alliances judged to be in the dynamic category— namely, Rover/Honda, ICL/Fujitsu and RBS/Santander— exhibited positive features in all three stages of formation, management and evolution. There were a small number of conflicting signals: the Rover/Honda alliance showed cultural problems in its early years; ICL/Fujitsu made no positive claims for its dispute resolution mechanisms; and RBS/Santander was not wholly convinced of the commitment of the middle management of the respective banks as those personnel were not closely involved in the alliance. All these alliances scored heavily on the proposed key variables, however, and were particularly strong on the evolutionary variable, including bonding and organizational learning.

SUMMARY

This chapter has provided a second form of classification for strategic alliances: namely, those that are *limited*, in that they are unlikely to develop further; those that are *latent*, i.e. they could develop further if certain behavioural or other constraints can be overcome; and those that are *dynamic*, i.e. that are currently prospering and seem likely to continue to do so. The case studies and statistical sample are then considered in relation to these classifications and to the qualities that are held to pertain to them.

11 Imperial Tobacco and Henri Wintermans

This and the following case study show how a failure to evolve consigns an alliance to the category of 'limited' effectiveness.

Imperial Tobacco had acted as the British agent for Henri Wintermans cigar company of the Netherlands ever since Wintermans was acquired by British American Tobacco in 1967. There was an agreement between Imperial and BAT, dating from the beginning of the century, that BAT would not sell in the UK other than through Imperial, and Imperial would not sell outside the UK. However, during the 1980s the relationship between Imperial and Wintermans deteriorated, as Imperial neglected its cigar business. It reached breaking point in 1988, but instead of breaking was regenerated by a new agreement in the form of a strategic alliance, whereby Imperial put new energy into its marketing of Wintermans' brands, and Wintermans assisted Imperial with technology to bring its cigar manufacturing up to date.

THE UK MARKET

The tobacco market as a whole has been under siege for some years owing to strong pressure from the health lobby, as evidence of the damaging effect of tobacco consumption on health has accelerated. Cigarette sales in the UK fell by 25 per cent in the period 1980–86, but since that time have levelled off, and then continued to decline as the government has raised taxes by more than the rate of inflation. The major tobacco companies have continued to be very profitable, as they have automated their production methods and increased their productivity. The level of the workforce in the industry is only one-third of the level 10 years ago. However, increasing restrictions on advertising and on smoking in the workplace have maintained the pressure on the industry.

The industry is strongly oligopolistic, with Gallaher (42 per cent), Imperial (35 per cent) and Rothmans (14 per cent) accounting for 91 per cent of all cigarette sales in the UK. Cigarettes account for nearly 90 per cent of tobacco sales, with cigars at nearly 4 per cent and pipe tobacco and roll your own (RYO) sharing the remainder.

Cigars sales have not fallen as dramatically as the sales of cigarettes, perhaps because their reputation for damage to health is not believed to be as great. However, this is probably due to the fact that more cigar smokers are light and occasional users. It is almost entirely a male-oriented activity, and the heavy users are virtually confined to the 35+ age group. The cigar market is worth about £360 million, and 75 per cent of this market is concentrated in small cigars. The brand leader is Gallaher's Hamlet with 40 per cent of the market. The remaining strong brands are all Imperial or Wintermans. Imperial's Castella Classic and Castella Panatella have 15 per cent and Wintermans' Cafe Creme has 11 per cent. Wintermans' total UK market share is 19 per cent.

IMPERIAL TOBACCO

Imperial Tobacco was founded in 1901 from a merger of a number of the leading British tobacco companies to meet a challenge from the giant American Tobacco Company which, having become No. 1 in the USA, was trying to repeat the process in the UK and Europe. Imperial was formed initially of 13 companies, of which the best known were W.D. & H.O. Wills, John Player & Sons, and Lambert and Butler. The companies formed an integrated company under one board of directors, but continued to trade under their own brand names.

In 1902 a truce was agreed, and Imperial and the newly

constituted British American Tobacco Company, of which Imperial was a major shareholder, agreed geographical spheres of interest. BAT stayed out of the UK and Imperial restricted its sales to the UK. Although various agreements and cross-shareholdings complicated the relationship over the next 80 years, the underlying principle was generally honoured, and BAT only manufactured in the UK for export, not for domestic sales.

In the 1960s, Imperial pursued a policy of diversification and expanded into food products, paper and board, drink and leisure, and in 1980 bought Howard Johnson hotel and restaurant chain in the USA. This proved its undoing, and after a number of years of falling profits, rationalization, and attempted alliances with potential partners, including United Biscuits, the group was acquired by Hanson in 1986.

Hanson proceeded, in characteristic fashion, to recoup much of the sales price by selling off many of the group's businesses outside the core business of tobacco. It then reorganized Imperial to increase its cost-effectiveness and efficiency. The Wills and Players salesforces were merged; the number of brands was cut from 155 to 63, and the number of packings from 238 to 105. This pruning continued until, in 1990, only 29 brands and 54 packings remained. A number of factories were closed or merged, and their technology modernized to improve unit costs,. The company was then divided into three strategic business units:

1.   Cigarettes and hand-rolling tobaccos
2.   Cigars
3.   Pipe tobacco and snuff.

The company consolidated its operations on three main sites in Bristol, Liverpool and Nottingham, and productivity increased very substantially.

HENRI WINTERMANS

The first Henri Wintermans cigar factory was founded in 1934 in Eersel in southern Holland. The company specialized in cigars, and was a family owned enterprise. In the 1950s it recognized the potential for export, and 600 million Henri Wintermans cigars now reach more than 100 countries. In the UK, Wintermans holds 80 per cent of the imported cigar market and accounts for 40 per cent of all Dutch cigar exports, with brands including Cafe Creme, Senoritas and Slim Panatella. In 1967 the company lost its independence and was acquired by BAT, which led to Imperial, in the time-honoured tradition, acquiring the UK distribution licence for Wintermans cigars.

EVOLUTION

From an agreement in which Imperial were the distributor for Wintermans in the UK, the 1988 negotiations turned the relationship into a real strategic alliance to which both companies contributed. It was to be a collaboration alliance without a joint venture company. Imperial agreed to give the Wintermans brands more active distribution effort, but at the same time they radically pruned the brands. Thus, from 30 cigar brands and 45 packings between Imperial and Wintermans the portfolio was reduced to 3 brands and 6 packings for Imperial, and 10 brands and 20 packings for Wintermans.

Wintermans have also enabled the Imperial cigar business to improve technologically. Cigar manufacturing was converted from a labour-intensive to a much more mechanized business by using large pre-prepared bobbins of leaf, prepared at low cost in the Dominican Republic, flown into Europe and fed into high-speed cigar-making machines. Imperial's productivity rose from 12 to 200 cigars a minute.

At Imperial the cigar business was the poor relation to the cigarette business. In 1987 cigarettes were making a 100 per cent return on capital, with a 40 per cent net margin. Cigars made 12 per cent on capital with a 5 per cent net margin. Clearly something had to happen to entice Imperial to stay in the cigar business.

The alliance agreement was set up in 1988 when relationships were poor. It included very specific market share objectives for Wintermans brands, and these have been exceeded. Objectives have been congruent in the short term, i.e. to revitalize the cigar market, improve profitability and take market share from Gallaher. However, in the longer term they may well conflict, as the opportunities for further growth may lead to cannibalization between the brands of the two companies.

Clive Inston of Imperial and his Wintermans' opposite number have played the 'gateway' role very effectively, and ensured smooth running of the relationship.

The cultural fit between the companies seems to have been good, but the entry of the BAT director to the Wintermans side may make this less easy in the future. The determined effort by the new Hanson-led Imperial team to show a positive attitude, to be committed, and to be trusting seems to have struck a chord with Wintermans, and has led to a dramatic improvement in relationships from their 1987 low. As Clive Inston says:

> Interestingly, since the changes at BAT, Wintermans seem to see us very much as allies in protecting their position in relation to their holding company; I don't think even two years ago they would have considered that possible.

The first activity following the conclusion of the alliance was brand reduction. This was achieved more successfully at Imperial than at Wintermans. Imperial believe there are still too many Wintermans brands and packings for the size of the market.

On marketing, Wintermans initially switched to the same advertising agent as Imperial, Lowe-Howard-Spink, in order to achieve a consistency of message. The changes at BAT led to Wintermans reverting to a BAT-sponsored advertising agent, and the Imperial salesforce was revitalized to put more effort into selling the Wintermans brands to achieve the agreed market share objectives.

On production, factories were rationalized and reduced to two for Wintermans and one for Imperial, and the Wintermans technical staff provided support to update Imperial's technology. Information was exchanged very openly in both the technical and marketing areas.

As a result of these activities Wintermans and Imperial cigars are both achieving a growing share of a declining market, and profits increased from £2 million in 1986 to £10 million in 1993. Wintermans brands represent about one-third of Imperial's cigar profit, and Imperial are responsible for about half of Wintermans' profits.

Despite a successful first stage, the current situation in the alliance is tense for a number of reasons. First, the two companies do not have a good strategic fit as they are both attacking the same market in the same way. The more successful each is in growing market share, the more are their objectives likely to clash as, ultimately, they cannot avoid taking market share from each other. Second, Wintermans' major contribution to the alliance—updating Imperial's technology—was a once-only activity. Imperial now has the technology and has no real further need of Wintermans in this area. Third, Wintermans owners, BAT, are changing their decentralization strategy and are becoming involved in Wintermans' activities. This may also lead to a clash of objectives with Imperial. The period prior to the renegotiation of the contract, therefore, may well lead to some considerable testing of the alliance equation, and to a review of who needs whom most, and how much. In this regard, Imperial, with its new technology and its slimmed down brand portfolio, seems to be in the stronger negotiating position. Opportunities for further evolution of the alliance are not obvious however, and this is likely to lead the alliance to be of relatively short term, with the partners ultimately going their separate ways.

SUMMARY

The question of the limited possibilities for the evolution of the alliance may place a restriction on its capacity for growth. Imperial and Wintermans may have no further prospects of increasing their shares in the UK cigar market unless they attack each others share. Also, the technology of both companies is now 'state of the art', and brand rationalization can probably go no further at Imperial, and not much further at Wintermans.

Inston talks of merging production units to achieve the greatest possible economies of scale; but this would be a difficult task unless they formed a formal joint venture company, and with Wintermans operating world-wide and Imperial only in the UK, this would present problems. Finally, the position of BAT as Wintermans owners may also represent a conflict of interest.

The alliance, therefore, having achieved its initial objectives with admirable effectiveness and positive attitudes, may be approaching the point when its strategic imperatives need to be reassessed, as these may no longer afford any obvious opportunities for evolution.

12 ICI Pharma

The joint venture between ICI Pharmaceuticals and Sumi-tomo Chemicals was set up in 1972, and is currently owned 60 per cent by ICI and 40 per cent by Sumitomo. It was named ICI Pharma (now renamed Zenecca Yakuhin KK following the ICI demerger), and was instigated by ICI because it felt the need to have a presence to market its pharmaceutical products in Japan. Japan is the second largest pharmaceutical market in the world after the USA, and it is very difficult to gain an effective presence there, except with a Japanese company as partner. ICI had made an earlier attempt to enter the market by granting licences to such companies as Daichi to distribute certain ICI products in Japan, but this arrangement limited ICI to a royalty stream, no bridgehead and no learning experience.

THE PHARMACEUTICAL INDUSTRY

The pharmaceutical industry has been one of the fastest growth industries globally over the last 40 years. Although the industry is fragmented in that the largest pharmaceutical company, Merck, has only 3.5 per cent of the world market and the top ten companies account for only 25 per cent, it is more concentrated in individual therapeutic areas and is dominated by large multinational companies. Only large companies have the resources to cope with the increasingly tight regulatory regimes that can cause a delay of up to 12 years between discovery of a new chemical entity and its full registration. A second factor, leading to dominance by large companies, is the need for very high R&D expenditures to discover truly novel drugs with clearly distinct qualities from those already on the market.

Two new features of current trends are evident. One is the growth of generic or OTC (over-the-counter) products which become available as the patents on proprietory products expire. The second is the entry of large companies from other industries—DuPont or Monsanto from chemicals, and Kodak, Nestlé or Procter and Gamble from consumer products—attracted by the high profit margins. These companies have large resources and may threaten existing pharmaceutical companies in the future.

Until recently, Japanese pharmaceutical manufacturers have been relatively insular, with their global presence limited to licensing arrangements and joint ventures. However, there have been a number of recent alliances that suggest that this may change: Takeda with Abbott in the USA, Eisai with Sandoz, and Dainippon with Rhône-Poulenc in Europe.

Currently the developed world, North America, Western Europe and Japan, account for 70 per cent of demand for pharmaceuticals, but for only 20 per cent of the world's population. Pharmaceuticals are therefore produced largely for rich countries. This will probably continue to be the case, but the globalization of the industry will increase as other regions, notably South-East Asia, succeeds in its economic development.

With the major changes described above taking place in the market, there is likely to be an emphasis on a number of major strategic factors: the development and maintenance of critical mass, globalization, specialization in limited therapeutic areas for research, and the increased development of strategic alliances. According to a recent survey by the Economist Intelligence Unit, there are few truly global firms. Only five firms operate on a worldwide basis, with production and R&D located in all three major market blocs. Another ten companies operate as multinationals with integrated operations in a smaller number of countries and two major R&D units. A further 20 have a core home country unit and then a multi-country system of mainly sales outlets.

Sixty-five operate selectively in a limited number of countries, and almost 7000 companies operate purely domestically, supplying local markets with repackaged and reformulated products.

ICI PHARMACEUTICALS

ICI Pharmaceuticals (currently demerged as part of Zeneca plc) was not the largest division of ICI. With a sales turnover of nearly £1.6 billion in 1991, it accounted for 13 per cent of group turnover, matched by ICI Paints, and exceeded by ICI Industrial Chemicals and ICI Materials. However, it was responsible for an overwhelming 52 per cent of the group's trading profit. To put this in perspective, the next most profitable division at ICI was Agrochemicals and Seeds, with 14 per cent.

ICI Pharmaceuticals has a strong portfolio of products focusing on the following therapeutic areas: cancer; infectious diseases; pulmonary, cardiovascular and arthritic diseases; disorders of the central nervous system; and metabolic illnesses. Despite its strong R&D competence, it has a policy of developing and marketing not only its own products but also licensed-in products from other manufacturers, and those involved in its joint venture arrangements.

Although a significant participant in the world pharmaceutical industry, ICI does not feature as one of the leading global competitors by market share on an overall basis. In 1991 it was the nineteenth largest company by value of sales with 1.4 per cent of the world market—about 40 per cent of the size of the market leader, Merck. The fragmented nature of the overall market is emphasized, however, in that even Merck had only a 3.5 per cent market share.

Given the need for pharmaceutical companies to specialize in particular therapeutic areas if they are to succeed, ICI has felt the need to fill out its portfolio with competitors' products and to seek partners in distribution and marketing arrangements around the world. This need reinforced its desire to set up its joint venture with Sumitomo Chemical in Japan. The driving reason was to attract a strong partner in

Japan. Sumitomo, otherwise, is rather weak in the pharmaceutical markets outside Japan.

FAILED EVOLUTION

As Barry Day, ICI Pharmaceuticals' corporate planner, stated:

> ICI's preference would have been to have gone for 100 per cent, but at the time it was precluded by law. But in Japan you need some presence in the distribution system to have any impact. You couldn't buy your way in, or go independent, so you had to get in with one of the big boys, e.g. Sumitomo, or Takeda, etc.

Under the agreement, ICI provided the product specification and raw materials, and Sumitomo handled registration, manufacture and distribution. The joint venture company was responsible for marketing and sales.

The ICI Pharma joint venture, doomed in many ways from the start, seems to have been a limited relationship. What Sumitomo had to offer ICI was some services of limited duration and geographical locus. When they had been performed for some time, ICI would inevitably develop its own ability to carry them out. The venture was also limited, because it applied only to Japan, and could not easily extend to other territories because of both companies' worldwide networks. Furthermore, ICI soon developed the view that, in the initial deal, Sumitomo had taken an unfair advantage by negotiating a manufacturing transfer price that was too high.

Looked at in more detail, the situation was as follows: in reward for its activities, Sumitomo received know-how and contacts that helped to develop it as a pharmaceutical company, the position of holding the Japanese registration for certain ICI products, a fee from ICI, and 40 per cent of the profits of ICI Pharma. ICI received 60 per cent of ICI Pharma's profit, but only after Sumitomo had taken a profitable fee from a number of activities, e.g. registration, manufacture and distribution. ICI was not able to achieve any real organizational learning, or any contacts or specific knowledge transfer, and became increasingly aware that cheaper options might well be available. ICI felt in summary that there was an imbalance in long-term rewards. When these factors are added to the facts that ICI retained its old licensing agreements in Japan, and that in comparison with the major domestic pharmaceutical companies the joint venture had no obvious competitive advantage, it is perhaps not surprising that the venture remained, at best, limited.

The attitudes that underlie the running of the alliance are also not conducive to a very successful project, at least not for ICI. First, ICI admits that it does not like alliances, and only enters them if there seems to be no other way to achieve the objectives. An ICI senior executive comments:

> Our present chairman is not so committed as our previous chairman. This may not harm the existing alliance, but it will affect the possibilities of extending the alliance to new developments. Our present chairman is concerned not to give the Japanese the chance to get in, and prefers unilateral arrangements like supplier agreements.

The cultural understanding does not seem to have been very effectively bridged, which limits the alliance effectiveness.

The president and chairman are appointed by ICI, the managing director by Sumitomo, and there is a full-time staff of about 800 Japanese nationals recruited locally, with a small number of ICI secondees. The company has developed its own culture to some extent—i.e. that of a foreign capital company, staffed mainly by Japanese, but therefore slightly outside the traditional areas where the best graduates seek jobs. ICI, despite 20 years in the joint venture, has still an uncertain understanding of the Japanese culture; as Barry Day says:

> One of the things that still holds us back in Japan is our lack of understanding of Japanese culture. Relationships are very important in Japan, and we are much less certain about what might spoil a relationship than we would be with a European or US company.

However, as Yoshiko Miyashita of ICI Japan says:

> As a result of the joint venture we have learned how to develop a pharmaceutical business in the Japanese market.

The joint venture was slow to develop a significant presence, since ICI did not take back any of its existing products from its old Japanese licensees, mainly because the registration rights belonged to the local manufacturing companies. However, in the 1980s ICI Pharma became the fastest growing of the non-Japanese pharmaceutical companies, and although it operates from a small base it has always been quite profitable. By 1990 ICI Pharma had about 1 per cent of the Japanese market, mainly in cardiovascular and cancer products, but it could still not compete on their home ground with the major Japanese companies, such as Takeda, Sankyo, Shionogi, Yamanouchi or Fujisawa.

A major factor impeding the development of the joint venture, and inhibiting ICI from putting more products through ICI Pharma, was the fact that, as mentioned above, the manufacturing transfer price from Sumitomo into ICI Pharma was too high and there was little profit left in the venture. In ICI's view Sumitomo was taking most of the profit at the manufacturing stage. As a result, ICI is now setting up its own pharmaceutical manufacturing plant in Japan to supply ICI Pharma. Also as ICI's experience increases in Japan, Sumitomo's regulatory, and distribution expertise becomes of less value to the venture.

A further limiting factor was the absence of new product flow from ICI research and the time-lag caused by slow development in Japan. This latter fact was partially the result of Japanese regulatory requirements, and the caution of Sumitomo and ICI Pharma in investing in products before they were seen to be registrable and saleable in the West.

The issue around manufacturing cost/margins was contentious: when the venture began, the unit manufacturing cost was high, and thus justified a significant fee to Sumitomo; however, as volume increased, the application of a simple percentage fee to Sumitomo probably rewarded them too generously. Furthermore, as the industry moved into the 1980s and 1990s, with enforced government price reductions in the UK, there was a reluctance by Sumitomo to accept equivalent reductions in the manufacturing fee.

ICI felt that the contributions of the partners therefore became unequal, and this made ICI unlikely to repeat the same method of having its products manufactured by Sumitomo. As an ICI senior executive comments:

> I think the relationship is good, but the issue is what do they bring to the deal? Some quality staff, a good Japanese name, people who are sound. On the distribution side your product gets into the package they distribute. You need that at the outset, but when you are established it doesn't matter any more. So our plan is to put new products into ICI Manufacturing, and then put them into ICI Pharma, but progressively we will change the distribution system and take more and more on ourselves.

Evolution depends on doing new things together, establishing common bonds, becoming learning organizations, and developing a mutual culture. Little seems to have been achieved in any of these areas in the ICI Pharma venture.

SUMMARY

ICI Pharma has developed a distinct culture that is not ICI and not Sumitomo; this is a common feature of joint ventures as they mature. However, as the lifeblood of a pharmaceutical company is its new products, and as these come only from ICI, then for ICI Pharma the staff attachment to ICI is the stronger.

The ICI Pharma joint venture has lasted for many years, and in the eyes of the partners it has met its measurable objectives and achieved a good reputation in the industry in Japan. Morale is also said to be high in the company, but the existence of the strong views described by the ICI personnel above is probably sufficient by itself to confine the alliance to the 'limited' category. In fact, the last word may well be left to a senior ICI executive as an epitaph to a limited alliance:

We have learned quite a lot from the Japanese, e.g. to simplify product design. The Japanese hang on your every word, and write it down. They are like blotting paper. When we spotted this we set out to baulk it; to be quietly obstructive!

13 Dynamic alliances—1 Rover and Honda

This and the following two chapters describe the strategic alliances that are judged to be *dynamic* in that they seem to reflect, to a great degree, the qualities and performance sought in an effective and successful strategic alliance. All three are collaborations.

BACKGROUND

The strategic alliance between the Rover Group and Honda was embarked upon after a meeting between the two companies at the Fairmont Hotel, San Francisco, in September 1978. The alliance is still in existence, although the decision of Rover's owners British Aerospace, to sell their 80 per cent holding in Rover to BMW threatens the continuance of the partnership in its present form.[*] Over its history the alliance has evolved from a limited licensing agreement to a multi-functional relationship including joint development and production, and a 20 per cent share exchange between the two companies.

[*] Subsequent to the case study research, Rover's parent company has sold its 80 per cent stake in Rover to a competitor, BMW, much to the apparent annoyance of Honda. This serves to demonstrate that commitment between the alliance partners may not of itself be sufficient if one or other alliance partner has a less committed majority shareholder. British Aerospace, Rover's majority shareholder, ran Rover at arm's length, and, as recent events demonstrate, did not therefore have the same depth of commitment as Rover to the Rover/Honda alliance. Nevertheless it has been announced that, despite this setback the collaboration is to continue, illustrating that strongly founded alliances can withstand strong buffetting without terminal rupture.

By 1978, Rover and Honda were approximately the same size in terms of world sales, with a turnover of almost £4 billion. Honda, however was profitable and growing rapidly, while Rover was making a loss and possessed factories that operated at a level substantially below capacity.

THE EUROPEAN MOTOR MARKET

By the end of the 1980s Europe had overtaken North America as the largest market for automobiles, with Germany, France, UK and Italy each responsible for more than 2 million annual vehicle registrations. Some major trends were noticeable: more choice was being demanded, and consequently more flexible manufacturing systems had to be employed; more sophisticated electronic equipment was being demanded and safety was becoming a selling feature. Although the Japanese had gained a very large share of the US market in the 1980s, they had penetrated Europe to a lesser extent. In 1990 they were estimated to have 11.6 per cent in total of the European market (Johnson and Scholes, 1993).

However, the Japanese were beginning to make their presence felt on the world automobile stage with their emphasis on quality, reliability, fuel economy, and robotic methods of manufacture. Among the Japanese car manufacturers, Honda was something of a maverick and an upstart. It had started its international life as a manufacturer of motorcycles and did not develop a presence in the car market until 1963. As early as 1978, however, Honda was surveying the European market as a new challenge. If it were to manufacture within the EC, its methods—short product life-cycle, low costs, roboticized manufacturing and high labour productivity—would give it a competitive advantage as the single European market took effect.

ROVER

At the outset Rover was an ailing car manufacturer owned reluctantly by the British government, and still making large losses despite the aggressive attempts by its then chief executive Michael Edwardes to modernize it through a major rationalization plan, and a determination to curb the trade union power that had contributed in a major way to make the company a sad example of failing British industry.

By 1978, despite the rationalization plan, the company was still losing money and was facing the prospect of a Conservative government less likely to continue to finance unprofitable development than its Labour predecessor. The world automobile market, after a number of years of growth, had plateaued, and increased market share, brought about by the ability to produce new models, was needed for success. Rover had been pinning its hopes on the Metro, the Maestro and the Montego, but none of these models was reaching its targeted sales figures, owing principally to Rover's reputation for somewhat variable quality.

At the very least Rover needed a new product in the lower medium market segment to fill a gap in its product range, but it lacked both the time and the finance to achieve this unaided. Still named the British Leyland Motor Corporation, the company was experiencing a declining market share, and seemed to have a bleak future. The world automobile industry was in a late mature stage, dominated by global giants. The economies of large-scale production and the marketing power of strong dealer networks, allied to good judgement in new model development, were the passport to success, and Rover had few of these key success factors in its armoury at that time. Rover lacked the financial resources and the time to produce new, market-acceptable models after the lacklustre performance of the Maestro and the Montego.

They also lacked a self-confident company culture after years of loss-making, union restrictive practices, disputes and poor press reports. They knew that they were regarded as one of the major 'lame ducks' of British industry.

HONDA

Honda was a successful company, but to the world automotive industry it was still regarded, principally, as a motor-cycle manufacturer. At the time the alliance was formed Honda's image was not sufficient to enable it to take its place naturally alongside General Motors in the US or Toyota in Japan. In fact, despite trebling its turnover during the 1980s, Honda is still not among the giants of the motor world. Also, in Europe its sales account for 1.2 per cent of the market, with Rover accounting for 3.1 per cent, against Volkswagen's 15 per cent and Ford of Europe's 14 per cent. Honda had established itself well in the USA, but of the three legs of the Triad, the European leg was to Honda almost entirely undeveloped in 1979. Also, Honda felt insecure in this area, and although it knew European tastes differed from those in America, it did not trust its understanding of those differences. Furthermore, Honda did not believe it had the time to develop its own European arm from scratch. The development costs of new European models would be too great at that stage of Honda's development, and the time scale too long to be acceptable. As Mr Hayashi, managing director of Honda UK, says:

> At that time there were restrictions on exports to Europe, therefore there was no way to increase our exports there. . . . Europe was suffering from over-capacity, so we had no chance to build our own factory there.

However, Honda had the characteristic Japanese 'Total Quality Control' attitude to manufacturing, which after a lengthy tuition period, was to elevate Rover into a quality performer. It had a pragmatic attitude to design that facilitated the creation of reliable marketable cars. It had the robotic methods of manufacture that could gain the necessary cost economies in unit terms. It had also sufficient finance to collaborate with Rover in the production of new models, and this was an important attraction.

FORMATION

The 1978 meeting in San Francisco took place because BLMC, as Rover then was, had recognized that if it wanted a successful future in the world automobile industry, it needed a partner. Roland Bertodo, Rover's strategic planning director, describes how the BLMC top management tackled the problem.

> We consciously sat down and wrote down all the automotive companies and listed the pluses and minuses against each one. Honda was the one that came out top purely because it was a similar size to us, it had growth ambitions, and a reputation for high quality at a time when quality for us was the biggest problem. It was renowned for its management at a time when we were struggling for management know-how. We were therefore attracted to Honda.

Honda responded positively to Rover's initiative, and the first deal was signed in December 1979, which was a limited licensing arrangement for BLMC to manufacture the Triumph Acclaim from Honda KD kits at the BLMC factory in Longbridge in Birmingham. The Triumph Acclaim was based on the Honda Accord and filled the vacant position in Rover's product range. Approximately 130 000 Acclaims were manufactured at Longbridge, and the brand achieved a regular position in the top ten UK sellers' list, although it was in reality no more than a re-badged Honda.

Rover had access to an acceptable UK and European network of component suppliers and subcontractors. It had ample spare capacity in its factories, and could manufacture as many cars for Honda as the Japanese company could manage to sell. Rover also had an understanding of European tastes, and it could contribute to the development costs of new models to make this necessary factor come within the financial reach of both companies.

The Rover/Honda alliance, therefore, began as a very limited arrangement in 1979, but as confidence grew between the partners, and they gained a realization of their respective qualities, the alliance matured into a much more involved collaboration. Rover was the driving force in bringing about the alliance, since as a government-owned 'lame duck', it desperately needed some passport to possible success. Honda's motivation was positive but probably weaker than Rover's. As Hayashi comments:

We thought the Rover approach might help in Europe. It was company policy to be flexible with people who approached us, and to have international collaboration, so we agreed to license Rover to manufacture Honda products from knock-down kits.

However, they covered any reservations they might have had by limiting the first deal to an arm's-length licensing arrangement, and some time later embarked on the building of the Honda Swindon factory to maintain their flexibility. Subject to these safeguards, their motivation was sufficient to enable the alliance to progress.

MANAGEMENT

Rover was slightly concerned in the beginning that Honda would take its know-how on European styling, and sourcing in particular, and walk away. As Bertodo says:

> We took steps to limit transparency and minimize informal transfer of knowledge by circumscribing a partner's opportunity to learn in an uncontrolled manner. . . . The challenge is sharing sufficient skill to create a competitive advantage for both partners while avoiding wholesale transfer of core abilities.

The risk from Rover's viewpoint was at shop-floor level, where such discipline was unlikely to prevail. Honda faced little risk in this area since, as John Bacchus, Rover's Director of Collaboration, commented, the Japanese are traditionally secretive by nature, and do not seem to feel the need to demonstrate their knowledge to show their abilities.

The 20 per cent share exchange, however, was made as a concrete demonstration of commitment. On this issue Hayashi comments that the share exchange was most important for the manufacturing and development staff, since it engendered trust, in that it showed that the partnership was for the long term.

Of course, the trust has not been naive. Rover has only released information on a 'need to know basis'; the Japanese have behaved similarly, and the two teams do not fraternize greatly at a social or shop-floor level. However, trust has developed as the two sides have become accustomed to working together. Matters moved on successfully and, as Hayashi says:

> The Legend, the joint Honda–Rover product, cleared the way for Honda to enter into the executive car sector of the market. Rover's interior design and European taste contributed to the success of the Legend. . . . Now Rover is a truly integral part of Honda's strategy in Europe.

Perhaps this is the strongest insurance for the survival of the alliance, i.e. the creation of joint assets that are key to the continuance of sustainable competitive advantage, and Rover/Honda seem to have achieved this. However, doubters see some cause for worry in over-dependence on the alliance for Rover. An article in *EIU Japanese Motor Business* (Bertodo, 1990) suggests that:

> model development in the car programme has been shifted over largely to Honda, with Rover manipulating the available hardware to encompass its upmarket and niche model ambitions. This compromise will permit a more rapid updating of the model range than Rover could otherwise contemplate but this attachment to Honda has also given rise to uninspired styling and uncompetitively bland designs.

Yet the alliance shows the strong commitment necessary for successful collaboration. As Hayashi says:

> We have strong commitment to the alliance. Even when we start production in Swindon we will still benefit from the joint supply network, and Rover is still in need of Honda's capability in product development, and quality standards. In that sense both companies have a management policy of strong commitment, because competition in Europe is very keen, and since we are already established in the UK with suppliers and co-operation with Rover this confirms our commitment.

Adaptation has probably been mainly on Rover's side, as it has painfully absorbed the successful Japanese method of operating large manufacturing companies. On contrasting cultures, Hayashi comments:

Much endeavour and patience were needed to overcome many barriers . . . in language, culture, ways of thinking and sense of value to name just a few. By overcoming these barriers, the people of Honda and Rover were able to generate mutual understanding and trust, which eventually led to close friendship.

As Bertodo confirms: 'Honda have compressed our learning curve and given us better value for money by sharing resources on R&D.'

There are joint design teams working on new models. The factories of both companies produce, or will produce, for the other partner. There is joint sourcing of components, and many compromises have been made to accommodate the respective manufacturing needs of the partners. The basic objectives of the partners are quite different: Rover sees its future as an up-market executive car niche marketeer, largely in Europe, while Honda has more global ambitions, but these objectives do not conflict.

EVOLUTION

The second phase of the partnership was the Rover 200 launched in 1984, of which 175 000 were built. This was the 'sister' model to the Honda Ballade. The 200 was basically a Japanese car with Rover fenders, wheels, bumpers and interior. The 200 and the Ballade were both produced at Longbridge and equipped with different badges. The agreement was more than a simple licence this time. Rover had the right to change the basic platform, and there was also a manufacturing agreement to make cars for Honda. The experience with the Ballade made the Japanese realize that Rover could provide the missing European values that Honda needed, and as a result helped to shape the way in which the relationship was to evolve.

In 1985, however, Honda announced its intention to build a factory in Swindon. This concerned the British Press as the question was raised as to whether this move heralded the decline of the alliance with Rover. This proved not to be the case. Honda proposed only to make engines in Swindon at first, and subsequently to make both Rovers and Hondas there. It was also mooted at this time that Honda might be in the market to buy Rover, but Honda claimed that it lacked the resources. It was concluded that this was not generally how Japanese companies behaved. Organic development was much more the rule than acquisition. By 1985 Honda was still a very small player on the British market. It sold 19 000 cars in the UK that year for 1 per cent of the market share.

In 1986 the partnership evolved further with the launch of the Rover 800 and the Honda Legend. This was the first car to be produced by a joint development effort. The experience of working closely together on design greatly enhanced the relationship between the two companies, and led to a substantial improvement in Rover's understanding of quality standards.

At this time Rover and Honda signed a statement of understanding to extend the partnership, which dealt with the principles of the relationship. However, it was felt that the mutual trust that had developed during the work on Project XX, as the 800 was called, was much more important than any legal document.

There was by this time a noticeable shortening in Rover's product life-cycle (see Figure 13.1). Also Rover's productivity was by now on a steeply improving curve (see Figure 13.2).

Honda insisted that it was not in the business of making excellent cars. Its aim was to make perfect cars! Some of this attitude was beginning to rub off on Rover.

A further maturing of the relationship occurred in 1988. Rover and Honda agreed to stop making the Rover 800 and the Honda Legend for each other at their respective factories. This was because both parties wanted to make refinements that could not be easily carried out at each other's factories. Honda had built only 1600 Rover 800s in Japan and Rover only 3500 Legends in Cowley. The decision did not damage the relationship in any way.

The next project, the Rover 200/400 with its twin the Honda Concerto, began in 1989. This heralded a further development, as this was the product of joint development

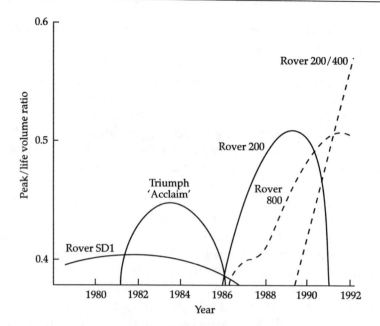

Figure 13.1   Progressive shortening of Rover product life-cycle

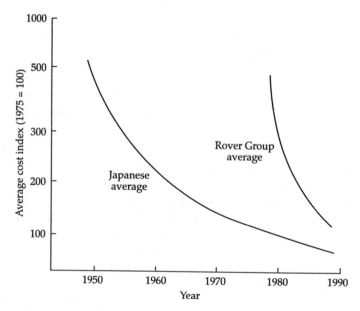

Figure 13.2   Comparative productivity experience

and co-production plus the cross-sourcing of components. Rover built more than 40 000 Concertos for Honda in 1990 to a quality standard acceptable to the Japanese. Rover and Honda are currently engaged on further collaborative ventures despite the sale of Rover to BMW, demonstrating perhaps the underlying strategic strength of the alliance.

Thus from an arm's-length licensing agreement in 1979 the alliance has made remarkable progress in terms of mutual development and production, and has even reached the point of minority share exchange. There has been no attempt to collaborate in merging marketing identity, or in management off the shop floor, however. Honda is still clearly a Japanese company with its own aims, ambitions and objectives, and Rover only features in these issues as a European partner. Similarly, Rover has its distinct identity, and shows no sign of losing it. The decision to continue marketing as separate entities can, however, lead to personality and identity problems. In early 1993 Rover launched the 600 series to fill the price gap between the 400 and the 800. Its twin is the Honda Accord. Honda announced:

> The largest selling Accord, the 2.0 iLS at £14 995 undercuts its near identical sister car, the Rover 620 SLi . . . and the Rover 620 SLi is not available with a driver's side airbag.

The Sunday Times of 11 April 1993 reported that a hasty retraction followed, deleting all references to Rover as a rival, as the announcement had breached the tacit agreement that neither manufacturer would criticize the other. All does not, therefore, necessarily go smoothly all the time.

Bertodo sees the alliance as requiring constant refreshing by both sides being ready with something extra to trade at each crucial point in what he calls the 'collaboration vortex' to prevent the alliance flying off certrifugally into independence, or centripetally into one-sided dependency. He sees a key part of his job as preventing Rover in particular from doing the latter. The key characteristics of bonding between the partners, commitment, trust and the development of the philosophy of the learning organization have all developed in large measure in the alliance, and it continues to evolve from year to year.

SUMMARY

The alliance has been very fruitful from the viewpoint of both partners. Alone, neither was a world-class motor manufacturer. Honda was strong in the USA and a medium-sized company in Japan. Its European presence was negligible. Rover was strong in Europe, but nowhere else. In fact 95 per cent of Rover's production in 1980 was for Europe, including the UK. However, together Rover/Honda now present a powerful world force with a strong presence in Japan, USA and Europe.

They were not alone in the world motor industry in forming alliances. In fact most major manufacturers have done so in recent years. Rover had some experience of disappointing alliances. As Bertodo recounts, they had been in fifteen previous alliances since 1921 with, among others, Isuzu, BMW, Ferguson, Hindustani, AMC, Perkins and, at the time of the Honda negotiations, Nissan. Only seven could be judged successful, he comments, and only four outstandingly so. However, from its position as a regular loss-maker, Rover has moved steadily into profit, and in 1990, as a subsidiary of British Aerospace plc, it contributed an annual profit in excess of £50 million to its parent, although the recent recession has reduced expected profits. For the past few years, sales turnover has been on a plateau at between £3 billion and £4 billion and its assets have shrunk dramatically from their bloated size in the 1970s. Rover's export sales have been reasonably stable in the late 1980s, but its UK sales are now expanding. It is now unashamedly a niche marketeer, as former chairman Sir Graham Day declared, and is no longer the largest UK car producer, coming third behind Ford and Vauxhall. Furthermore, the Honda-related models still account for only about one-quarter of total production. The much maligned Metro, Maestro and Montego are still responsible for a substantial tranche of Rover's sales. Nonetheless, the Honda alliance has had a dramatic effect on

Rover's quality performance, and it is no longer viewed as a 'loser'.

Honda has grown from a medium-sized company in 1978 with a turnover of around £4 billion to one with a world-wide sales level of more than £12 billion—of which 66 per cent is earned outside Japan—and a net profit after tax of more than 500 million in 1990. Not all of this can be attributed to the alliance with Rover since Honda was already strong in the USA at the time the alliance was formed, and motor-cycles, power products and parts account for a quarter of total revenue. However, in Europe, the most relevant area, Honda's sales of cars have increased from a negligible amount in 1978 to £700 million or 191 000 units in 1990. Not only have Honda raised their European direct sales but they also benefit from part of Rover's approximately 450 000 unit sales.

If quality and a regenerated reputation were prime objectives for Rover, these seem to have been established. The 800, the 200 and the 400 series are all generally acknowledged to be first-class cars from a quality viewpoint, and Rover's reputation is reflected in its profit figures. It is estimated also that the inter-company business between the two companies is currently worth almost £500 000 annually. As Hayashi comments:

> If we broke apart, we would be in competition with the same technology, the same components, the same suppliers, and the same products: a duplicate of ourselves.

This is perhaps a fitting epilogue to a collaboration that has grown and evolved over more than a decade to the considerable benefit of both partners but without compromising the identity of either. In an interview in 1991, Bertodo summed up the relationship in the most picturesque way: 'We have a shared bed, but we dream separate dreams.'

14 Dynamic alliances—2   RBS and Banco Santander

On 3 October 1988 the Royal Bank of Scotland and Banco Santander of Spain announced plans for a wide range of commercial co-operation. The Royal Bank ranked as Britain's sixth largest bank after the 'Big 4'—Lloyd's, Barclays, National Westminster and the Midland—plus the more international Standard Chartered Bank.

Banco Santander ranked third in Spain in terms of profits. Both banks wished to position themselves in the new situation created by the European Single Market due to be fully established by the end of 1992. As the *Financial Times* commented next day, in reaction to the announcement of the establishment of the alliances:

> Yesterday's alliance between Royal Bank of Scotland and Banco Santander of Spain is a bold bid by two relatively small banks to stake out a place for themselves in the unified European financial markets after 1992.

THE EUROPEAN BANKING INDUSTRY

At the time, the major European banks were aware that the Single Market Act would sweep away many of the national barriers that had been protecting them in their domestic economies and impeding their internationalization. However, by 1988 there had been little cross-border merger activity by the banks to herald major structural competitive changes in the industry.

Five major deals had been concluded, Deutsche/Banca

d'America and São Paulo/Hambros in 1986, São Paulo/Suez in 1987, and Amro/Generale and Midland/Euromobilare in 1988. This list was not long, although the list of minority link-ups would be considerably longer.

Revolution in the banking world did not seem imminent therefore, but there was much discussion, and the general conclusions were that European banking would take over from national banking and the structure that emerged would favour the large supermarket banks with their extensive networks and great scale economies leading to low unit costs of transactions through adoption of cutting-edge technology. It was also considered that there would be a place for niche banks, so-called 'boutiques' whose higher costs would be compensated for by more personal service, and specialist skills in specific low-volume areas not so subject to automation.

THE ROYAL BANK OF SCOTLAND

In 1988 The Royal Bank Group, whose major asset was the clearing bank, The Royal Bank of Scotland (RBS), was a broadly based financial services group with total assets in excess of £20 billion and profits before taxation in 1987 of approximately £200 million. RBS is a retail bank which accounted for 80 per cent of the group's profits; it had 850 branches throughout Great Britain but with its history and its head office in Edinburgh, Scotland was and remains its strongest domain. RBS was merged in 1985 with the group's English subsidiary, Williams and Glyns. Other activities of the group included merchant banking through Charterhouse plc, financial services through Roy Scot Finance Group plc, investment management through Capital House Investment Management Limited, insurance through Direct Line and travel through A.T. Mays plc. The Royal Bank Group has subsequently bought Citizens Bank of Rhode Island, USA, which, with assets of £4 billion, is currently the second largest bank based in Rhode Island. The Royal Bank Group is a proud old Scottish-based institution which traces its roots back more than 250 years.

Although the thrust of the alliance with Banco Santander was to be mainly in RBS's area of activities, a cross-shareholding, initial contacts and negotiations were set up at group level. At the time of the alliance, the Royal Bank Group was one of the most profitable banking groups in the UK, but was more dependent on the UK economy than its major competitors, and typically was awarded a smaller share of the international business of its corporate clients. A further area of vulnerability might have been seen as the 15 per cent stake held in the group by the Kuwait Investment Office. A major launch into Europe was not a possibility owing to lack of financial muscle; the development of individual offices across EC countries did not present a feasible option; and there was a reluctance to have major rights issues. Niche acquisitions, however, were a possibility.

BANCO SANTANDER GROUP

Banco Santander is also a bank of ancient lineage and ranks highly in the Spanish banking system on a number of counts; in 1988 it was fourth largest in terms of deposits with total assets of £15 billion, the third largest in terms of net income with £200 million pre-tax profits in 1987, and with over 1450 branches it had the largest branch network of all the Spanish banks. It was a leader in Europe in developing electronic off-site banking by telex, telephone, personal computer and video. The Santander Group also provides a broad range of financial services, including investment banking, investment management and insurance. Although it is predominantly a Spanish domestic bank, it has a number of activities outside Spain, and a number of agencies and representative offices. It regards itself as an international bank, since these offices make a significant profit contribution.

FORMATION

Some time prior to 3 October 1988, RBS had reviewed its priorities in Europe and decided that the top priority was to enhance its domestic customer base by developing its capability to service European needs. Second, it wished to create new profit-generating customer bases in Europe. Any consequent enhancement of RBS's prospects of remaining independent was merely an added bonus.

It assessed its strengths and weakness, and the opportunities and threats in the European market. It identified opportunities in plastics, life assurance, development capital, private banking, car insurance and fleet management. It was particularly attracted by Spain, France and Germany, and it noted the large British expatriate community in Spain in particular. Believing that it would require a partner to capitalize on any of these opportunities, it began a screening process, looking for *inter alia* a banking group of similar size with prima facie compatibility of culture and activities. It was determined to adopt a low-risk and a low-cost strategy if at all possible, and for these purposes the alliance route seemed the most attractive.

Santander emerged at the head of the list of possible partners, and after initial favourable contacts by the Royal Bank Group, bilateral working parties were set up, which, working to a tight time schedule, produced a Memorandum of Understanding by August. As a matter of coincidence, at the time of the initial contact by the Royal Bank Group, Santander were simultaneously approaching the Royal Bank Group through other channels. The legal aspects of the proposed alliance were then dealt with, and a series of basic rules were agreed, setting out how each partner should act in each other's country. The basic rules encapsulated the spirit of the alliance. This was followed by the task of selling the alliance to the shareholders, staff, press and the analysts.

From the outset the alliance was complex, but it was agreed that it would be limited to two partners and would be a wide-ranging collaboration of many activities. It was felt that the formation of a joint venture company as the primary vehicle for the alliance would be too limiting and inflexible, and that the more robust collaborative form was more appropriate in the circumstances. The major areas of co-operation envisaged at the time of the alliance announcement are listed below.

Access to branches

The major link between the clearing activities of the two banks involved establishing an RBS presence throughout Santander's Spanish network, and a Santander presence in the RBS's major UK city branches. The purpose of this was reciprocal: to enhance the service the partners could provide in each other's countries for multinationals, expatriates and tourists. The primary functions were to be advisory services, money transfer, domestic and foreign currency loans, cash dispensing and off-shore banking.

Shared ownership of German and Belgian banks

Santander sold to RBS 50 per cent of CC-Bank in western Germany, and of Credit du Nord Belge. CC-Bank had 35 branches and total assets of £342 million. It is primarily a consumer finance house. Credit du Nord Belge had 22 branches and assets of £320 million. Although RBS was to be equally represented on the boards of these two banks, Santander continued to manage them.

Off-shore banking in Gibraltar

A 50–50 banking joint venture was to be established in Gibraltar, marketed through the branch networks of the two partners with the objectives of meeting the financial needs of the expatriate community in southern Spain and Gibraltar. It was agreed that RBS would manage the joint venture, since it had the stronger link with the target customer base.

Merchant banking

The merchant banks of both groups—Charterhouse plc and Banco Santander de Negocios—were to co-operate on stock-broker, securities placement, leveraged buy-outs and merger and acquisition activities, principally in Spain and the UK.

Charterhouse was sold in early 1993 to CCF Bank of France and BHF of Germany. As CCF is already part of the international funds transfer network (IBOS) established through the alliance, it is well known to the partners. There are already direct links in terms of flows of business between RBS and Banco Santander de Negocios; therefore this relationship is not disturbed by the Charterhouse divestment.

Technology development

Co-operation was planned, on a cost-sharing basis, to develop technology to provide better services to meet customer needs at a wide range of locations throughout Europe. Priority areas were identified as electronic home banking, self-service terminals, and enhanced branch technology.

Acquisitions

It was appreciated that the alliance, as defined, would not be adequate to meet the criteria for a wider, European, banking enterprise. The partners therefore declared themselves ready to consider joint acquisitions to provide a physical presence in countries where neither group had access to a branch network. Each new venture was to be managed by either Banco Santander or by the Royal Bank Group, depending on the nature of the business and its location.

The alliance was predominantly in the form of a complex collaboration. However, mainly as an act of faith and a demonstration of commitment, small percentage shareholdings were exchanged at group level. The Royal Bank Group bought 2.5 per cent of Banco Santander. Santander bought 2.5 per cent of the Royal Bank Group's equity, and, in addition, purchased a further 2.5 per cent that was then held by the Kuwait Investment Office (KIO). In December 1988, three months later, Santander bought a further 5 per cent from the KIO, thereby raising its shareholding in the Royal Bank Group to almost 10 per cent, and making it the bank's largest shareholder. The two banking groups placed directors on each other's boards, and the boards committed themselves, through the alliance, to:

(a)   develop profitable customer bases in Europe;
(b)   provide services to corporate and personal customers of both groups through a large number of outlets in Europe;
(c)   market improved cross-border financial services.

The decisions at formation seem to have been well prepared and wisely taken. The collaborative form was chosen because of the wide and flexible range of activities to be carried out together. However, the existence of two smaller businesses in Belgium and Germany, and subsequent developments in Gibraltar, caused the partners to adopt the joint venture form for these activities, but to allocate prime responsibility for management to one partner or the other to avoid confusion in day-to-day control. The consortium form was also adopted for the development of the IBOS system through the setting up of a European Economic Interest Group (EEIG). However, the founding partners drive IBOS particularly from a technological point of view as the management company is owned by both partners.

The driving forces behind the creation of the alliance were, predominantly, the lack of size and international standing of the partners in the face of the regionalization of the banking industry, presaged by the European Single Market Act. In partner selection the allies concentrated on similar size, similar range of activities, relatively similar cultures and lack of conflicting objectives. Both were determined to remain independent and not select a partner who would ultimately take them over.

MANAGEMENT

In order to manage the relationship effectively, a high-level surveillance committee—meeting every six weeks and comprising the group chief executives and strategy directors of both banks—was formed to review progress and priorities, and Santander was in the process of installing a video-conferencing link with the Royal Bank Group's existing video system in London and Edinburgh. At an operational level the Royal Bank Group held internal fortnightly meetings to review progress, and the RBS established a small new unit to implement practical elements of the alliance. Subsequently, an annual costing process was to be introduced to ensure that the costs of running the alliance were roughly balanced between the two partners.

It was soon found that the way the alliance had been negotiated posed problems for its implementation and management because of the Royal Bank Group's structure. The negotiations with Banco Santander had taken place exclusively at group level, although working parties were mainly at bank level. RBS, which was the institution most intimately involved in the alliance, had therefore found ownership of projects difficult to assimilate. Fortunately, a restructuring of the group into business units had the side benefit of eliminating the bank/group element as a potential difficulty. Bank personnel were subsequently appointed to key committees, which overcame the 'ownership' problem.

The Royal Bank Group's chief executive, Charles Winter, declared in July 1989:

> It is already clear that broadly based co-operation between RBGS and Banco Santander will have significant impact on the long-term strategic evolution of both groups. The alliance reduces the cost to both sides of researching markets outside its own and of establishing a presence in such markets. It also reduces the risks associated with such geographic diversification.

He also added contemplatively:

> We have been surprised by the intangible benefits from the alliance as each side has got to know and observed the working practices of the other. Simple things like the differing ways in which we prepare and organize meetings; the nature and content of papers presented to internal audiences; and differences in structures and reporting relationships have all provided ample food for thought.

On the question of culture, RBS had some surprises. They discovered that Santander took much longer to answer letters, operated much more by word of mouth than by memo, and had different attitudes to credit risk. This last was not of itself surprising, but what was surprising was the extent to which customers assumed that the partner bank would replicate without question the credit assessment of the RBS on its customers.

The Spanish partner was also more concerned with the protocol of seating arrangements at meetings and dinners. On the other hand, as Jose Saavedra of Santander commented, it was also discovered that RBS was meticulous in committing everything to paper, and in considering matters very carefully before acting. Santander is more action oriented and, having a chairman who is also a major shareholder, is inclined to make immediate decisions. However, an attitude of tolerating differences, adapting to them and learning where possible, prevented cultural differences becoming a problem.

The key attitudes of trust and commitment were present from the beginning at the top, and Santander's willingness to reduce the less comfortable KIO shareholding created a strong bond from the outset. The trust has continued to develop, with the result that each partner is quite content to permit the other to represent its interests in appropriate third party negotiations and other activities connected with the alliance.

In the management systems area, initial decisions were not quite so happy. The Royal Bank Group did not give RBS sufficient involvement in the beginning and a number of detailed cultural differences seem to have caused surprise and a little irritation between the partners, although time has led to improvements and greater understanding in both areas. Attitudes seem to have been very positive from the start, especially at the top, and bonding activities of a conscious and unconscious nature have helped further on this front. The cultural issues hinted at by Charles Winter were soon generally understood and now represent no more than interesting anecdotal information. Working together has led to considerable bonding among the key participants, which has benefited the alliance in a major way. As Saavedra comments again, commitment and cultural adjustment are strong at the top and at the bottom, where there have been personnel secondments of Royal personnel to Santander. However, in the middle levels of the organizations—i.e. the branches—mutual understanding is less developed as the foreign partner is often seen to disturb the domestic priorities of middle management.

Since the alliance was formed, the top structure has changed slightly as relations are now directly between the banks and not the groups, and Walter Stewart at RBS and Jose Saavedra at Banco Santander are established as the 'gateways' through which all alliance traffic from branches, departments and customers pass, and if it does not pass that way, it is at least copied for information. This developed system has been found to be beneficial, and serves to avoid, or at least to mitigate, the misunderstandings to which numerous uncoordinated and random interfacing between the partners might tend to lead. However, as Saavedra points out, the ultimate aim must be to evolve to a position of cultural understanding where the 'gateway' withers away, and to that end departments of similar interests are encouraged to work together (e.g. international, franchising, marketing, technology and credit) for mutual business interests and to share expertise.

EVOLUTION

Six months after the public announcement of the commencement of the alliance, RBS made a progress report as follows:

1. Services had been set up for RBS personal customers at 50 Santander branches, with an initial group of five secondees sent to work over the summer in Santander branches; and for Santander customers at the RBS's London Knightsbridge branch from Summer 1989.

2. For corporate customers, RBS had appointed coordinators in London, Manchester and Glasgow and a general

manager in Madrid. Santander had appointed a corporate customer coordinator in London.

3. Santander had set up a franchising and licensing unit in Madrid to assist companies to set up intercountry licensing agreements within Europe. This matched that of RBS, which had a significant presence and expertise in that market.

4. RBS cash-line cards could be used in Santander in-branch ATMs, allowing customers to draw pesetas on their British account, and Santander issued a student card for use in RBS's ATMs.

5. The jointly owned Gibraltar bank set up under the RBS name was to open in August, 1989.

6. A venture fund was being established. Initial funding of £25 million was being raised, of which the partners were each contributing £5 million.

7. Co-operation between the merchant banks had been established and two major management buy-outs were carried out together in Spain.

8. On technology, the International Banking Organization Services (IBOS) system was to be launched. It would allow customers to gain access to their accounts from any part of the alliance branch network.

The principal evolutionary event in the development of the alliance, however, was the announcement of the plan for an electronic banking network across Europe. This presaged the later development of the IBOS system that was to become so important to the development of the alliance. It was to prove to be the alliance's most innovative and dramatic instrument. The system was intended to cure the lengthening delays in international money transfers, and to obviate the need for a central European clearing house. The system allows customers of both banks to transfer funds between Britain and Spain on the same day; to arrange for standing orders and direct debits overseas; and to obtain statements. It was announced in *The Times* at the end of 1990 that the partners were negotiating with French and German banks to extend the network, and already planned to include Banco de Commercio e Industria SA of Portugal, which was controlled by Santander and The Royal Bank. Dr George Mathewson, appointed chief executive of The Royal Bank Group in 1992, said that he expected a wide number of corporate and personal customers to use the service. The consortium to be set up to operate IBOS on a Europe-wide basis would be an EEIG (colloquially known as an Earwig), with a legal structure based on the French *groupement d'intérêt économique*, and adopted in European Community law.

The evolution of the IBOS system as a potential source of pan-European competitive advantage has given considerable impetus to the development and importance of the alliance to the two banks. To put it in perspective, however, IBOS is still small in terms of volume and transactions since, until 1993, it was restricted to individual customers. The corporate sector has yet to be attached. In the absence of IBOS, however, it might be questioned whether an undoubtedly successful relationship from a human relations standpoint would lead to sufficient sustainable competitive advantage to make the alliance and its partners clear likely winners in a Europe without national barriers in the financial services area. Among the executives interviewed, all regard the alliance as a success, at least from a subjective viewpoint. As in all alliances of the collaborative form, clear statistics of alliance achievements are difficult to determine, since a successful relationship leads to great organizational learning, and this does not always reveal itself in predictable numerical form. However, the partners are aware of this and are actively attempting henceforth to quantify alliance results by the adoption of a range of output measures.

The activity of the business has tended to go predominantly one way, i.e. north to south. While UK corporate customers have extended their activities into Spain, there has been little reverse flow. The income has therefore gone mainly to the Spanish partner; but other activities have been undertaken on behalf of the partner that would not have been available had it not been for the alliance. RBS has benefited in its service provision to international corporate customers, and this is recognized, although it is more difficult to quantify. However, the alliance executives are currently attempting to quantify targets and achievements more systematically than they did at the outset of the alliance. They see competitive advantage in being able to offer a potential customer access to over 8000 branches, with more to come through the IBOS system, and this is now seen as the greatest development of the alliance. CCF of France has also joined the IBOS system.

SUMMARY

The situation in RBS at the time the case study was written was similar to that in all British clearing banks in the midst of a very deep recession. The Report and Accounts for the year ending 30 September 1991 showed profits before taxation down to £57 million from £262 million in 1990, lower levels of commercial activity, and bad debt provisions having taken their toll. However, the 1992 accounts showed substantial improvement.

It is clear from the accounts that the alliance with Banco Santander is, directly in terms of profit generation, only of relatively minor importance in the totality of the bank's activities, but it is nevertheless a very successful venture from the co-operation viewpoint, represents a considerable increase in RBS's European standing, and through IBOS has placed two fairly small banks at the technological cutting edge of banking applications. As a by-product the alliance has considerably strengthened RBS's ability to serve its customers in Central and South America.

It is clear that any thoughts of European acquisitions are now in the past, as the alliance partners have learned that, through the extension of IBOS, they can achieve all they wish on the European scene without the added expenditure and risk of acquisition.

Jose Saavedra of Santander lists some of the benefits that have been gained as a result of the alliance:

We have learned how best to launch an interest bearing current account after having learned what RBS's experience has been. We admire how they develop business by phone, even selling loans. At top management level we are exchanging views on how best to handle credits, and geographical risks. On the Royal side, they look at our branch network with 5 people or less per branch, and compare it with their average of 9. Probably they will centralize the back office more. Also they are very good at serving customers, and we are very good at developing profitable customers. As time goes on something more consistent will come out of the cocktail shaker. But those are processes that are on-going and enriching on both sides.

Over the life of the alliance there has been considerable evolution of the relationship. Most of the activity areas set out at the beginning are now well established. The IBOS system is developing more rapidly than had been envisaged; staff are being exchanged on secondment to the other partner; and a number of anecdotal incidents and, in general, close working have led to a high degree of bonding between all the executives involved. There are also plans for the future. Saavedra talks of developing IBOS so that it is not purely European. He sees a potential role for the system on a global basis, including future members in at least the USA and Japan, so that customers of RBS and Santander can have a truly worldwide funds transfer service with unique speed and efficiency.

However, only the future will tell whether the mature development of the Single Market in financial services will leave the alliance partners strong enough to compete with the major European 'supermarket' banks, or whether adequate niches will develop to avoid the need for head-on competition. Furthermore, both banks are domestic banks in essence, and to put two domestic banks together does not create an international bank, as this requires different types of teams, possibly a wider range of services, and perhaps a different culture. The partners to the alliance always envisaged that they would remain as individual banks rather than create a unified bank. So it must remain an open question, over the next few years at least, whether even a successful alliance could possibly still fall between the two stools of being neither sufficiently specialist for a niche bank, nor sufficiently large for a major Euro-bank.

15 Dynamic alliances—3   ICL and Fujitsu

The alliance between ICL and Fujitsu has developed gradually over a decade, being first initiated in October 1981 as a technology collaboration. The relationship developed further, however, during the 1980s until Fujitsu bought 80 per cent of ICL's equity in 1990. Fujitsu chose to regard the relationship as a collaborative alliance rather than an acquisition, and plan to float a substantial part of their holding of ICL on the London Stock Exchange before 1995. As ICL chairman Peter Bonfield mentioned to *The Sunday Times* (1 December 1991):

> Fujitsu realises that its style of management is not the ICL style. They understand that the best way to protect their investment in ICL is to let ICL function as an autonomous public company within the Fujitsu family

THE COMPUTER INDUSTRY

The computer industry is undergoing dramatic structural change. Having become a global industry, within which no national producer is safe, its boundaries have become blurred with those of other industries, and its operating segments have also been transformed. It is now perhaps more appropriate to think of an information industry than a computer industry. The industry in which Fujitsu defines itself encompasses computer manufacturers, software development companies, telecommunications companies and semiconductor or microchip manufacturers and provides the major parts of the supply structure to the information industry.

The traditional segments have also broken down. In the early 1980s the industry divided fairly logically into companies producing hardware or software. The hardware companies supplied the business sector largely with mainframe and mini-computers and the personal sector with personal computers. All this has changed with the advent of area networks and open systems architecture. Multiple workstations are challenging mainframes in the business environment, and the personal area is fragmenting into desktop PCs, laptops and notebook computers. Meanwhile the major manufacturers are diversifying their offerings. IBM is now both a hardware and a software company, and is not limited to a software alliance with MicroSoft. Fujitsu, the world's second largest computer company, operates in the areas of hardware, software, telecommunications and microchip manufacture. Meanwhile, PC hardware has become a commodity, with 'no-name' manufacturers accounting for over 40 per cent of the market, and the major manufacturers each holding only small market shares. IBM, the market leader in PCs, has only 13 per cent of the market and Apple, the no. 2, has only 7 per cent. Mainframes have become an over-mature market in which, rather than buy a new mainframe, most major companies are more concerned with developing a method that enables their various computer systems to interact with each other.

The route to sustainable competitive advantage has become ever more difficult to determine, and the world recession and cessation of growth in the industry has caused most major computer companies, even IBM and Fujitsu, to record losses. In Europe in 1992, Bull, Olivetti and Siemens were all in loss situations, and only ICL was still showing a profit, aided by the resources of Fujitsu.

In an attempt to cope with this structural change, the industry is beginning to federate on a major scale. The three major European manufacturers, Bull, Olivetti and Siemens-Nixdorf, have created a new joint venture company to build what they call a European 'nervous system'. IBM had de-integrated from a tightly organized vertical structure into a looser federal one, and has set up a wide-ranging alliance with Apple Corporation. Fujitsu has built a world computer enterprise including ICL and Amdahl of the USA. While this has increased the flexibility of the industry, some commentators claim it has done nothing to aid the re-establishment of its stability.

ICL

ICL is Britain's largest computer company and has, during its somewhat chequered history, been supported by the government at different times to help it attempt to mount a British challenge to IBM, largely in the mainframe segment of the computer market. It was formed in 1968 from a merger of English Electric Computers and ICT. In 1984 it was acquired by STC with the aim of forming one of Europe's leading communications and information systems groups, but STC lacked the resources to achieve this perhaps over-challenging objective.

In 1990, Fujitsu took an 80 per cent shareholding in ICL, and in 1991 ICL merged with Nokia Data, thereby strengthening its continental European operations. ICL now supplies hardware, software and services to over 70 countries of the world. It is strong in retail systems in the UK, France, Italy, Australia and Sweden, and a leading supplier to public administration throughout Europe.

On the product side, ICL is dedicated to open systems, and was one of the first companies to anticipate the emergence of those systems in the market. ICL is no longer restricted to mainframes, and has a fast-developing range of PCs, including laptops. It has also recently launched a software partners programme to enable software producers to develop and market their software for ICL platforms. In 1990, ICL became the first information technology (IT) company to achieve company-wide accreditation in the UK to the ISO 9001 Quality Systems standard.

Until its link-up with Fujitsu, it has never really looked like a winner in the increasingly competitive global computer market. Since its alliance with Fujitsu in the early 1980s, however, ICL has become consistently profitable. In 1991 its revenues reached almost £2 billion, and its pre-tax profit £62 million. Even in the midst of the world recession in 1992, it was still showing a profit.

FUJITSU

The Fujitsu Group with revenues of approximately $21 billion is second only to IBM with $67 billion in the list of global IT companies. However, at the beginning of the 1980s IBM was 40 times the size of Fujitsu, so despite its considerable size advantage, IBM looks back to a dominant past and a less certain or secure future, facing the challenge of Fujitsu and other Japanese-based enterprises.

Fujitsu's strategy is to develop associations and technical alliances with leading IT companies across the world to build a global network of outstanding technical and marketing strength and flexibility: the Fujitsu 'family'. Fujitsu recognizes that the driving forces in the electronics industry mostly involve reductions in size and weight, and is therefore concentrating on the low size end of the market, with notebook PCs, palmtop Japanese word processors and cellular telephones. At the same time it does not neglect mainframes, and in open systems is promoting the world-wide standardization of the UNIX operating system.

The major areas in which Fujitsu operates are:

1. *Information processing.* Fujitsu is the Japanese number 1 in the small computer market. It is also a significant competitor for fax machines, open systems, software, and LAN and VAN systems.
2. *Telecommunications.* Fujitsu is a major supplier to NTT, Japan's premier telecommunications company. It is also strong in the field of mobile communications and digital switching systems. It is a leader in the field of high-speed optical transmission technologies, and a major supplier to NTT in this area also.
3. *Electronic devices.* Fujitsu produces 4 and 16 Mbit DRAMs as its major memory products. It is also a major

producer of compound semiconductors, a fast-expanding area. It is very strong, and is at the forefront of development in R&D in the electronics industry in its key sectors.

FORMATION

In 1980 ICL was under severe pressure. It had realized that small computers, particularly personal computers (PCs), were beginning to dominate the market, but it was traditionally a mainframe producer and lacked the financial resources to cope with product development in both mainframes and PCs. It was therefore actively seeking a complementary partner, and after screening a number of possibilities it identified Fujitsu as most closely meeting its needs. The collaboration was to be more than an original equipment manufacturer (OEM) arrangement, and was to include technological co-operation as well as increased volume sales of components such as the 700 series microprocessors from Fujitsu.

This agreement transformed ICL's fortunes as it could now maintain its profitable mainframe business and commit, with Fujitsu, adequate development resources to the new opportunity area of open systems. In June 1984 the agreement was extended to include co-operation on software, and this was to continue until 1991. ICL had by then developed a new strategy, which involved focus on a few European geographical markets and on certain specialist segments, namely office automation, defence, retail stores and local government. Collaboration with major foreign companies was also to be an important plank of its strategy.

This strategy, including the collaboration with Fujitsu, continued successfully throughout the 1980s. However, in 1985 ICL was acquired by STC, which itself was still 25 per cent owned by ITT. As a result, STC began to drain ICL of its development funds in order to finance its precarious position in the telecommunications business. ICL therefore commenced discussions with the STC board with a view to gaining its independence. Talks with STC and other companies continued through 1988–89, and eventually in July 1990 an agreement was reached in which Fujitsu purchased 80 per cent of ICL, leaving Northern Telecoms (which had in the meantime purchased STC) with the remaining 20 per cent. It was agreed that 49 per cent of the company would be refloated within five years; therefore, ICL did not become a subsidiary of Fujitsu and the relationship remained a collaborative strategic alliance.

The basic form of the alliance is that of a complex collaboration. Co-operation reigns in a number of areas, and where joint ventures are considered to be appropriate—as in North America, Australia and continental Europe—these have been formed to provide focus for clear business areas outside the core geographical areas of the two partners. The collaborative form is slightly unusual for an alliance in that Fujitsu have acquired 80 per cent of ICL's equity, with a view to reducing this stake to 51 per cent within five years. In these circumstances, Fujitsu might have been expected to have consolidated ICL into the Fujitsu Group as a subsidiary. However, they preferred to allow ICL to remain autonomous, and to enable the alliance to develop by negotiation and agreement rather than by fiat, in the belief that this would lead to the more effective development of the joint enterprise. In 1991, the chairman of Fujitsu, Takuma Yamamoto, stated:

> ICL continues to be run autonomously as a European-based Information Technology Company. We believe that, in this partnership, the growth of ICL is growth of the Fujitsu Group as well.

The motivation for the alliance internally was ICL's need for a financially strong partner to help fund its development, and Fujitsu's recognition of ICL's capacity to help it realize its global ambitions. Externally the globalization of the industry, the speed of technological change, and the opportunities for scale economies were reasons for co-operation.

Partner selection was dominated by the recognition of the possible synergies in the two companies. Mr Kitazato, Fujitsu's resident UK manager of coordination and liaison sums up the identified synergies:

ICL's strengths are in open systems, total systems capability, its market driven approach, its drive towards industry standardization, and with Nokia Data in ergonomics. Fujitsu's strengths are in semiconductor technology, the integration of computers and telecommunications technology, its capability as a total IT systems supplier, and in basic research in advanced technology.

The ICL corporate culture was also appreciated in its practice of open management and communications, its speed of response, its customer orientation, and in its concern for quality. These were all features that Fujitsu valued and, in the speed of response, felt they could learn from.

MANAGEMENT

The management of the alliance involves a small number of Fujitsu executives based at ICL's Putney headquarters in a liaison role. As is often the case with Japanese companies, no very specific dispute resolution mechanism was created. However, the management of the alliance has generally been good, since overall objectives are in harmony, and mutual attitudes are very supportive. In the content analysis of the interviews it can be seen that information dissemination is regarded by the executives interviewed as particularly good between the two companies.

The *Guardian* (31 May 1990) reported that prior to the establishment of the alliance, as early as the spring of 1980, a group of ICL executives embarked on a brainstorming session. They sought free association of words with a randomly chosen word 'heart'. Their first effort revealed their paranoia towards the Japanese challenge in their industry; they chose words like DAGGER, HEART ATTACK and DEATH. Then they relaxed and became more positive with LOVE, CHILDREN, HAPPINESS and MARRIAGE. It was with the latter attitude that they approached the Fujitsu alliance, which paid dividends as trust and commitment met with trust and commitment on the other side.

EVOLUTION

The evolution of the alliance has been strong, as is shown in the joint ventures set up around the world. Bonding was strong from the beginning, since Fujitsu not only came to ICL's rescue when it was in a very precarious ownership position with STC, but also allowed the British company to retain its autonomy in management.

As seems to be the case in most alliances with Japanese partners, constant learning has been a key feature of the relationship. In particular, ICL have learned to provide the Japanese level of quality and customer service, and to take responsibility for results in an individual's own area of business after having agreed matters consensually. On the Fujitsu side, the Japanese company admits to having been hit by the big company disease, as shown in the following comments in the Fujitsu company newspaper:

The Big Company Disease has the following symptoms:

- Frequently heard remarks: 'There are no such precedents', 'It does not suit our company', 'The rules do not allow us to do this'.
- Meetings with no decisions.
- Avoidance of risk-taking work.
- No quick response, no quick action.
- Numerous papers being prepared for internal use only.

ICL does not suffer from this, and Fujitsu admits to learning to move more quickly and more effectively as a result of exposure to ICL's management approach.

Fujitsu also owns 49 per cent of Amdahl in the USA, and the three companies, Fujitsu, ICL and Amdahl, proceeded to set up a joint product strategy group to develop systems to meet the opportunities presented by the market's moves towards open systems architecture. This was consistent with the vision of Takuma Yamamoto, chairman of Fujitsu, who believed that the industry of tomorrow was likely to be characterized by networks of companies tied into borderless strategic alliances. In fact Fujitsu's declared strategy is to build a federated global organization with the necessary skills and flexibility to become a global market leader.

This declared strategy was not, however, believed by the increasingly paranoid European computer manufacturers, and ICL was unceremoniously expelled from a number of European research consortia, notably JESSI, the Joint European Submicron Silicon Initiative, who nonetheless allowed the American IBM to join.

Fujitsu proceeded to develop its global strategy in concert with ICL. In October 1991 Nokia Data, the leading IT company in Scandinavia, was merged into ICL increasing the company's operating strength in Scandinavia in particular. In April 1992 Fujitsu–ICL Systems Inc. was set up (80 per cent ICL owned; 20 per cent Fujitsu) out of the North American retail businesses of the two companies, and placed under ICL's management control. In the Pacific area, Fujitsu Australia Limited was created out of both companies' Australian interests (80 per cent Fujitsu, and 20 per cent ICL) and in continental Europe, Fujitsu Systems Business—Europe was created to bring Fujitsu's supercomputer and M-Series general-purpose computer systems business in Europe under ICL's management control.

The worldwide recession has been particularly severe on the Japanese market, and Fujitsu recorded a pre-tax loss of $78 million in the half year to September 1992. To put the matter in perspective, IBM also recorded a loss during that year, the first in their history. ICL, however, are profitable, and it is not believed that difficulties in Fujitsu will affect the plan to float ICL when market conditions are right, probably in 1995.

SUMMARY

The alliance is very successful, both internally within the companies and externally within the industry. The only factor in the long-term prognosis that does not point in the right direction is that of balance. Clearly Fujitsu has the ultimate power, owing to its ownership and financial strength. This unbalancing factor could affect the alliance negatively, if the present colleagues in the operation of the alliance change over time, since many commentators suggest that the most durable alliances are those that have an approximate balance between the respective strengths of the partners. However, Killing's research (1983) suggests that alliances with one dominant partner may well be most successful, as a possible source of power ambiguity is thereby avoided. In that event the prognosis for the ICL/Fujitsu alliance is good.

16 Partner relationships: the key to success

This, the final chapter, tries to draw some general conclusions on how best to form and manage a strategic alliance. The conclusions are quite widely based, having emerged from a close look at ten established alliances, and from statistical analysis of 67 alliances. The main conclusion from both strands of the investigation is that partner relationships are more important as a predictor of a successful alliance than any other economic, organizational or structural factors.

The ten case studies demonstrate that, for an alliance to be formed, some external driver is needed in order to make potential partners aware of their resource dependency needs and vulnerabilities. The nature of the external force may vary, as may the nature of the resource dependency, but to set the process in motion, both must exist and be perceived. Partners are always selected on the basis that they are perceived to have complementary assets, and that it is believed that synergies can be achieved from joining the value chains of the partners. Cultural fit, however important it may be eventually, is rarely explicitly considered in the choice of partner.

The management of the alliance is a crucial element in determining its effectiveness, and here congruent non-conflicting objectives are important, as are clear organizational arrangements. Cultural sensitivity also plays a significant part, especially in the boundary-spanning activity. The most effective alliances display positive attitudes of commitment and trust between the partners, and strong personal relationships, i.e. bonding is established between personnel from partner companies most closely involved in the alliance.

Alliances that are effective over the longer term show some

evolution—i.e. new responsibilities and new projects are assigned to them, and the partner companies display organizational learning to a high degree. If the alliance is to display long-term effectiveness, it is important that one partner does not benefit at the expense of the other, and that one partner does not become too dependent on the other.

The statistical part of the investigation changes the focus of the conclusions slightly, by emphasizing the specific association of particular factors with alliance effectiveness. For example, because virtually all respondents claimed that (a) their alliances used asset complementarity and synergies as partner selection criteria, (b) they had selected the right alliance form and (c) they had generally compatible objectives, these hypothetically important variables failed to show discriminatory qualities in the statistical analysis when correlated against the success of the alliance, although their importance emerges more strongly in the case study analysis. However, this did not affect the classifications of the case studies into the categories of limited, latent and dynamic.

The statistical analysis also gives pointers on the relative importance of the variables—a factor that is difficult to determine from interviews. Congruent long-term objectives, for example, are highlighted as very important in the case study research, but the statistical findings relegate this variable to second-order (though certainly not low) significance.

The cluster analysis suggests that the evolutionary variables have an interrelated structure of their own. Thus, individually they are necessary but not sufficient to affect the outcome of the alliance, but together they provide an effective recipe for alliance development. Organizational learning is therefore very important to the evolutionary dynamic of the alliance, but this in turn must be supported by a substantial degree of bonding between the partners if an effective alliance is to result. On reflection, this is sensible, since organizational learning alone may lead to more knowledgeable partners who no longer feel the need for an ally. A flexible attitude to change does, however, show a strong direct relationship to alliance effectiveness.

The cluster analysis reveals, on the other hand, that the management variables are each more directly tied to alliance effectiveness than they are to each other. Thus, positive partner attitudes, clear organizational arrangements, and cultural sensitivity do not reveal a strong internal structure with each other. The importance of these variables is confirmed, however, in the statistical analysis, having been observed in the qualitative research.

The third important conclusion from the cluster analysis is the link between globalization and the realization of scale/scope economies, and the direct link between these motivational factors and alliance effectiveness. It is clear that these two factors are contingent rather than universal variables, but that at this point in economic history they are of prime importance in stimulating alliance formation, and, if handled appropriately, in creating the conditions for effective alliances. Obviously, at other times in history, alliances may be stimulated and realized by other dominant factors.

POSITIVE CONCLUSIONS

Key positive conclusions from the study are:

1. The most common current motivations for alliance formation proved to be, externally the globalization of markets and the growth of fast-changing technologies, and, internally, the need for specific resources and competencies to be able to thrive and survive in these markets, including the size to achieve the economies of scale and/or scope made available as a result of globalization. Partners were chosen, therefore, with these factors in mind.
2. Although cultural compatibility was rarely a major consideration in selecting a partner, sensitivity to culture at least was found to be a very important factor in predicting alliance effectiveness.
3. Of the three identified stages of alliance development—namely, formation, management and evolution—the statistical analysis suggested that the formation conditions and decisions were the least associated with the ultimate effectiveness of the alliances.

4.   However, positive attitudes in managing the alliance, and actions to stimulate bonding and organizational learning during the evolution of the alliance, were strongly associated with its effectiveness.

5.   The cluster analysis showed that integrated partner behaviour—covering, in particular, organizational learning, positive alliance expansion of role, and bonding—represented a powerful formula for the maintenance of an effective alliance. On the management side, positive attitudes, cultural sensitivity and clear organizational arrangements were each seen as important.

6.   It was clearly shown that international strategic alliances need not be transitory arrangements between resource-deficient firms who consider themselves to be actually or potentially in trouble. Of the 67 alliances researched, 20 per cent were founded more than 10 years ago, with Dow/Corning the oldest with a founding date in 1943. This is a sufficiently large percentage to dispel the label of transitory arrangement.

This research project was carried out from the positive hypothesis that alliances can be effective, potentially long-term, organizational arrangements between companies, and can lead to sustainable competitive advantage that is not easily achievable by the partners separately.

The cases reveal in detail how alliances between firms can lead to very effective federated enterprises. However, the single most important contribution that emerged from considering 10 alliances in depth and a further 57 by questionnaire was probably that *Positive Partner Attitudes* was the major key to an effective alliance. Such a variable covers a wide variety of behavioural attitudes. It is particularly associated with the attributes of commitment both at the top and in middle management, in trust between the partners, and in the exhibition of cultural sensitivity. It is also strongly associated with partner bonding, flexibility in response to change, particularly concerning partner objectives, and to a willingness actively to bring about the evolution of the alliance. It would seem that this single set of attitudes

represents the strongest predictor of the effective development of a strategic alliance.

The 'hard' factors in the equation—e.g. structural form,
specific resource dependencies, transaction costs, and synergies—may be important as underlying economic factors with
'ecological' power, but the overall presence of turbulence and
uncertainty in the environment may well prevent the
economists' concept of the force moving all situations
towards equilibrium from having much influence on the
outcome of alliances. Survival is a much more important
dynamic, and this needs to be reassessed with each turbulent
change in the environment. Flexibility, then, may be a much
more important quality than having the least cost organizational form at all times. If this is indeed the case, as the
preponderance of respondents seem to believe, the power of
positive attitudes may well win the day for inter-firm
collaboration, even for alliances with prima facie limited
strategic synergy.

IMPLICATIONS FOR MANAGEMENT

If the above conclusions are valid, the implications for
executives considering embarking on a strategic alliance are
considerable. They suggest that the principles outlined in
Roehl and Truitt's view that 'Stormy open marriages are
better' (1987) are unlikely to be true in the longer term.
Furthermore, Reich and Mankin's attitude in 'Joint ventures
with Japan give away our future' (1986) is unlikely, if carried
into an alliance, to lead to a successful joint endeavour.
Alliance negotiations heavily attended by corporate lawyers
also set a bad atmosphere for a subsequent trusting operation.

Over-tight concern to gain more benefits from the alliance
than one's partner may well be self-defeating in the end; and
too narrow and restrictive an attitude towards allowing the
partner access to systems and markets is unlikely to stimulate
bonding.

There was little evidence from the exercise to suggest that
the selection of alliance form is in any way crucial to its
effectiveness. The case studies, however, suggest that joint

ventures that are not endowed with a full set of assets to stimulate their autonomous development may be needlessly handicapped. In all cases boundary-spanning activity should be a subject of major concern, since this is the area in which the venture may exhibit its greatest potential tensions.

The research also suggests that the believed identification of very strong complementary resource dependency needs and synergies is no predictor of an effective alliance. The research does not seek to claim the validity of two stronger statements, i.e. (1) alliances can be effective without complementary assets or synergies, or (2) strategic fit, or the potential for competitive advantage achieved jointly but not separately, is not necessary for an effective alliance. Such statements would probably be too counter-intuitive to be case study credible, and are not borne out by the insights from the analysis where flexible growth based on evolution and the economies of scale and/or scope, achieved in an atmosphere of mutual trust, is shown to be a most important factor.

The positive implications for management are, however, quite unambiguous. They indicate that

- *if positive attitudes of commitment, trust and cultural sensitivity are adopted,*
- *if clear organizational arrangements are made, particularly those involved in the boundary-spanning activity,*
- *if organizational learning by both sides, and not mere competence substitution, is seen as the fundamental objective of the alliance,*
- *if the alliance is allowed to evolve, and*
- *if a major effort is made by the partners to achieve strong interpersonal relationships, including bonding and flexibility to changing arrangements,*

then an effective alliance is probable.

Such an alliance may be put forward as the 'ideal' model for international strategic alliances, and embodies the key characteristics that emerged from the study of 67 international alliances formed over a period exceeding 10 years, encompassing many varied organizational arrangements and covering a very wide range of industries.

Appendix A: the questionnaire

This appendix contains an uncompleted example of the questionnaire used to obtain quantitative data from the 67 alliances in the research.

INTERNATIONAL STRATEGIC ALLIANCE QUESTIONNAIRE

The aim of this research is to gain a greater understanding of why firms develop strategic alliances and how they run them. The questionnaire should not take more than fifteen minutes to complete.

A *strategic alliance* is defined as a co-operative arrangement between organizations in which the partners make substantial investments in developing a long-term collaborative effort and common orientation.

1. An alliance may be *focused* on a specific objective, or *complex* involving a more general co-operative agenda between the partners.
2. An alliance may involve the creation of a jointly owned new company, i.e. a *joint venture*, or it may be a flexible *collaboration*.
3. An alliance may involve only *two partners*, or it may be a *consortium*.

Alliances will in all cases involve some combination of the above three factors.

Name of Alliance executive completing Questionnaire:

Address:

Telephone number:

Company and position:

Date:

Alliance partners:

Date of formation of alliance:

Industry served by alliance:

Purpose of alliance:

Nature of Alliance form:

1.   (A) focused or
      (B) complex scope
2.   (A) separate joint venture company or
      (B) flexible collaboration
3.   (A) two-partner alliance or
      (B) multi-partner consortium

Please circle (A) or (B) in each case

International Strategic Alliances
Questionnaire

Please record the strength of your agreement or disagreement with each statement on the scale of 1 to 5.

Please answer 1a, 1b or 1c, dependent upon which basic form was chosen for the alliance. Note: a consortium joint venture is classified as a consortium.

Please answer from the viewpoint of the alliance as you perceive it, not from the viewpoint of just one partner.

			Strongly disagree				Strongly agree
1a		The alliance was concluded in the form of a joint venture company because:					
	1a(i)	the alliance scope constituted a distinct business	1	2	3	4	5
	1a(ii)	the assets involved in the alliance were specific to it	1	2	3	4	5
	1a(iii)	the assets involved were easily separable from the partners' other assets	1	2	3	4	5
	1a(iv)	the assets needed to be jointly managed	1	2	3	4	5
	1a(v)	the achievement of the objectives of the alliance could be clearly measured in relation to the use of the alliance assets	1	2	3	4	5
	1a(vi)	there was a perceived need to tie in the partners	1	2	3	4	5
	1a(vii)	it was legally necessary, e.g. to get into a new market	1	2	3	4	5
	1a(viii)	the partners wished to allocate only a predetermined level of resources to the venture	1	2	3	4	5

1b	The alliance was set up as a collaboration, i.e. without a separate joint venture company, because:

			Strongly disagree				Strongly agree
1b(i)	there was considerable uncertainty as to what tasks would be involved in the joint enterprise		1	2	3	4	5
1b(ii)	the partners wished to retain flexibility, and therefore did not wish to create a new legal entity		1	2	3	4	5
1b(iii)	visible commitment by the partners was not sought		1	2	3	4	5
1b(iv)	the alliance boundaries did not describe a distinct business area		1	2	3	4	5

1c   The alliance was set up as a consortium because:

1c(i)	two partners could not provide sufficient resources to meet the needs of the opportunity		1	2	3	4	5
1c(ii)	large size was necessary for the enterprise to be credible to potential customers, e.g. governments		1	2	3	4	5
1c(iii)	the specialist skills required were so wide and varied that more than two companies were necessary		1	2	3	4	5

1c(iv)	extensive geographical coverage was needed to achieve strong market presence	1	2	3	4	5
1c(v)	there was a need to spread and limit the financial risk to each partner	1	2	3	4	5

2. A key motivation for forming the alliance for one or other partner was to gain:

2a	technology or know-how	1	2	3	4	5
2b	key labour skills	1	2	3	4	5
2c	local knowledge to enable entry to new markets	1	2	3	4	5
2d	raw materials	1	2	3	4	5
2e	marketing skills	1	2	3	4	5
2f	distribution chanels	1	2	3	4	5
2g	managerial skills	1	2	3	4	5
2h	brand names	1	2	3	4	5
2i	reputation and general image	1	2	3	4	5
2j	legal requirements	1	2	3	4	5

3. A key motivation for the alliance for one or other partner was to spread the financial risk

       1   2   3   4   5

4. A key motivation for the alliance for one or other partner was to be able to get to the market fast, and thus not miss an opportunity

       1   2   3   4   5

		Strongly disagree				Strongly agree
5.	An alliance was chosen, because it was the least cost solution	1	2	3	4	5

Note: Cost in this sense must be broadly interpreted. For example, it would be very high cost if the alliance led to loss of proprietary expertise due to appropriation of skills and assets by our partner.

			Strongly disagree				Strongly agree
6.		The following factors in our industry were influential, leading to the formation of the strategic alliance:					
	6a	turbulence in markets	1	2	3	4	5
	6b	economies of scale and/or scope enabling the largest producers to achieve the lowest costs	1	2	3	4	5
	6c	globalization of the industry	1	2	3	4	5
	6d	regionalization (e.g. EC) of the industry	1	2	3	4	5
	6e	fast technological change leading to ever-increasing new investment requirements	1	2	3	4	5
	6f	shortening product life-cycles	1	2	3	4	5
	6g	high economic uncertainty	1	2	3	4	5

7.		The partners selected each other largely because:					
	7a	they had complementary assets	1	2	3	4	5

7b	there were possible synergies perceived in working together	1	2	3	4	5
7c	the partners were of an approximately similar size and strength	1	2	3	4	5
7d	their culture was compatible with each other	1	2	3	4	5

8. The partners are achieving their alliance objectives to a degree acceptable to them

8a	in direct quantifiable terms	1	2	3	4	5
8b	in more indirect spin-off terms	1	2	3	4	5

9. The alliance is run by means of very workable organizational arrangements, notably:

9a	good dispute resolution mechanisms	1	2	3	4	5
9b	clear authority in the hands of the managing director in a joint venture	1	2	3	4	5
9c	an appropriate alliance form	1	2	3	4	5
9d	a divorce mechanism agreed at the outset	1	2	3	4	5
9e	information concerning the alliance, disseminated widely in the company	1	2	3	4	5

		Strongly disagree				Strongly agree
10.	The long-term goals of the partners are not in conflict	1	2	3	4	5
11.	The partners have positive attitudes towards the alliance notably:					
11a	a sensitive attitude to national cultural differences	1	2	3	4	5
11b	a sensitive attitude to corporate cultural differences	1	2	3	4	5
11c	strong commitment by top management	1	2	3	4	5
11d	strong commitment at lower levels	1	2	3	4	5
11e	mutual trust	1	2	3	4	5
11f	internal morale regarding the alliance is high amongst all levels of personnel involved in the alliance	1	2	3	4	5
12.	The alliance is constantly evolving, in that:					
12a	the partners are regularly coming up with new projects for the alliance	1	2	3	4	5
12b	additional responsibilities are being placed on the alliance	1	2	3	4	5
12c	the alliance is constantly adjusting to change	1	2	3	4	5

13. One partner has not:

13a	gained strategic advantage over the other	1	2	3	4	5
13b	gained greater benefit than the others	1	2	3	4	5
13c	become over-dependent on the other	1	2	3	4	5

14. Strong bonding factors have developed in the alliance. The partners have

14a	successfully gone through an external challenge together	1	2	3	4	5
14b	exchanged personnel successfully at a number of levels in the partner companies or in the joint venture	1	2	3	4	5
14c	developed a mutual culture that is a combination of the best of the partners' cultures	1	2	3	4	5
14d	developed a good reputation in the partner companies	1	2	3	4	5

15. The partners are adopting a philosophy of constant learning in relation to the development of the alliance:

			Strongly disagree				Strongly agree
	15a	the partners have set up systems to disseminate learning throughout the partner companies	1	2·	3	4	5
	15b	the partners individually review what they have learned from the alliance	1	2	3	4	5
	15c	the partners regularly review what they can learn next from their partner	1	2	3	4	5
16.		The reputation of the alliance is good in the industry	1	2	3	4	5

Appendix B: the statistical findings

This appendix sets out the detail of the statistical part of the research. The questionnaire sample obtained was a quota sample which, for the strict statistician, precludes generalization to the total population of alliances, since the size of such a population cannot accurately be known. However, it is still helpful to look at the patterns of association between the classifications in the data-set, and to infer from them the aspects that contributed most towards the effective development of the alliance. At the very least these inferences constitute robust hypotheses for further exploration.

Structured statements relating to the propositions had been developed in the questionnaire (see Appendix A), in which the respondents were requested to select possible answers on a five point ordinal Likert scale running from 'strongly disagree' to 'strongly agree'. The questions were based on issues identified in the literature, plus further issues arising in the qualitative interviewing in the 10 case studies. The resulting data from 67 alliances are multiple classifications of each alliance, according to the perceptions of each questionnaire respondent. The independence of the informants, and the nature of the questions and resulting classifications, permitted the examination of associations between (a) the criteria upon which each alliance is classified and (b) the perceived effectiveness of the alliance.

THE DATA

The 67 alliances were formed over a lengthy period in the last half century. The majority were founded in the last 10 years, however, and all are international in that there is at least one non-UK partner, or they are operating in the international market. There are no known accepted statistics registering all international alliances formed over the period, although some researchers have attempted to estimate new alliance formation involving the larger companies by noting their citation in the press.

The taxonomy described in the body of the book was applied to the sample, and breakdown was found to be 54 per cent joint ventures, 32 per cent collaborations and 14 per cent consortia.

The sample of 67 cases covered a very wide and varied range of alliances. All eight categories of the taxonomy were represented; 36 industries were covered, with the largest numbers of cases from one industry being Financial Services with 8 and Telecommunications with 6. Partners from 18 nations were represented, and the period of duration of the alliances varied widely. Twenty per cent had been in existence over 10 years, 13 per cent between 5 and 10 years, 34 per cent between 3 and 5 years and 33 per cent less than 3 years.

The questionnaire is structured in a hierarchical form with the dependent variable *effectiveness* operationalized by 5 questions. The questionnaire contains 82 questions operationalizing the 15 variables.

The data-set comprises two blocks of information:

1. Data drawn from the in-depth case studies ($n=10$). For these cases there were, on average, four respondents for each alliance. To classify these alliances on each criterion average responses were calculated.
2. Single responses from a further 57 alliances.

The questionnaire (see Appendix A) is seeking to test propositions in relation to:

- reasons for the selection of particular alliances forms
- motives for setting up alliances
- criteria influencing choice of partner and their impact on alliance effectiveness

- conditions and attitudes that may lead to the effective management and development of alliances.

The development of an alliance has been analysed in relation to three phases:

- *Formation* (questions 1 to 7)—The independent variables are:

  Q1a–c the form of alliance
  Q2   internal motivation
  Q3   risk motivation
  Q4   speed-to-market motivation
  Q5   cost motivation
  Q6   external factors motivation
  Q7   partner selection criteria

- *Management* (questions 9 to 11)—The independent variables are:

  Q9   organization systems
  Q10   congruence of long-term goals
  Q11   partner attitudes

- *Evolution* (questions 12 to 15)—The independent variables are:

  Q12   alliance development
  Q13   balanced partner benefits
  Q14   bonding factors
  Q15   learning philosophy

Five questions are randomly placed in the questionnaire and represent an index of the *dependent variable* alliance effectiveness. These are questions Q8a, 8b, 11f, 14d and 16. Answers to these questions are averaged to produce an overall effectiveness rating (Q16ag), i.e. the aggregate of the five effectiveness questions averaged.

Where appropriate and feasible, the *independent variables* have been operationalized by posing a number of detailed specific questions. Indices for each variable have been constructed by taking the mean of the scores on the relevant questions. Thus, scores on Q7, for example, have been computed by averaging the answers to Q7a–d. Exceptions to this practice are as follows:

1. In questions 3, 4, 5 and 10 no operationalized questions were considered necessary because of the specific nature of the variables.
2. In questions 2 and 6, internal and external factors that may have led to alliance formation have been listed. Clearly, only certain factors will be appropriate here in each case. Any of the motivations may be sufficient to stimulate alliance formation, but no one may individually be necessary. Therefore, only the identified factors (i.e. those scoring 4 or 5 on the Likert scale) have been averaged to get a figure for Q2 and Q6.
3. Question 8 has not been averaged, since 8a and 8b have the same status as the other operationalized questions pertaining to the dependent variable *effectiveness*, and this is averaged in Q16ag.

In view of the limited sample size, and the large number of variables, and in order to maximize the reliability and validity of a complex multi-level multi-variate analysis, all the responses were dichotomized from the Likert scale such that 1 and 2 were recoded as 1 and 3–5 as 2. The midpoint was thus included in the positive category, as recommended in *Research Methods in Social Relations* (Johoda *et al.*, 1951). It was felt that the effectiveness scale needed greater graduation, and for this variable the 5-point Likert scale was collapsed into 1, 2 and 3.

OBJECTIVES

The objectives of the statistical analysis are as follows:

1. To identify reasons for the selection of particular alliance forms.

2. To identify the most common motives for alliance formation.
3. To establish a possible relationship between alliance motivation and alliance effectiveness.
4. To establish a possible relationship between alliance form and alliance effectiveness.
5. To establish a possible relationship between partner selection criteria and alliance effectiveness.
6. To establish possible relationships between the management and evolution variables and alliance effectiveness.
7. To establish the underlying structure of the variables and show how they relate to each other.

Objectives 1 and 2 can be met by analysing frequency distributions for the answers given to questions 1a–c and 2–6, respectively, in the completed questionnaires.

Objectives 3–6 require an analysis of the level of statistical association between variables. This analysis has been guided by two general null-hypotheses, namely:

NULL-HYPOTHESIS 1: *There is no significant association between alliance form, the identified motives for alliance formation, or the adoption of the identified partner selection criteria and alliance effectiveness.*

NULL-HYPOTHESIS 2: *There is no significant association between the identified management and evolution variables and effectiveness.*

Some insights into the nature of objective 7 can be achieved by means of cluster analysis carried out on those variables that are found to be significantly associated with alliance effectiveness.

STATISTICAL METHOD

Simple frequency distribution analysis was used to establish the level of cited reasons for the selection of an alliance form, motives for alliances formation, and the most common partner selection criteria. For the associational analysis, parametric statistical methods of multiple or step regression were judged to be inappropriate to the data analysis for a number of reasons; for example, the sample was relatively small, the data were ordinal, the total population was not known, and assumptions of a normal distribution could not confidently be made. The non-parametric 'Chi-square' test was therefore selected to test the significance of the difference between (a) the observed frequencies of association among the independent and dependent variables, and (b) the frequencies expected under the conditions of the null-hypothesis. 'Somers d' was used as a directional non-parametric measure of association between the independent variables and the dependent variable, as described by Cohen and Holliday (1982):

> Somers d is an asymmetrical measure of association; that is to say it is appropriate when we wish to predict order on y from order on x.

A cluster analysis was then carried out on the variables significantly associated with effectiveness in order to establish whether the associational relationships were directly with the dependent variable, or whether the variable relationships were more complex. The non-parametric cluster analysis technique was employed as detailed in McQuitty (1957) to provide a clear visual interpretation of the patterns of association in the matrix. For the present purposes, it is argued that combining Somers d with McQuitty's simple and robust analytical method provides the best possible solution within the limitations of the data-set.

After performing the dichotomization process described above, the resulting matrix (82 × 82) was inspected for patterns of association, and for each cell a cross-tabulation was tested by the chi-square method, with appropriate corrections for small cell size (Yates and Fishers correction). According to Cohen and Holliday (1982):

> The stability of the test is said to be decreased if there are less than 5 expected frequencies in any category or cell.

The resulting matrix of associations was examined (a) to

eliminate vectors carrying no information, (b) to eliminate possible redundancies between variables, i.e. where an association was so high and so consistent across other variables as to suggest auto-correlation, and (c) to identify areas of association with the pre-defined dependent variable.

The data were run on the SPSS software package, cross-tabulating the 14 variables individually against the effectiveness variable, and computing chi-square and Somers d values. The exercise was then repeated for all 82 variables, including the operationalized ones, in order to identify possible associations at a more specific level. Chi-square and Somers d values were also calculated at this level. With two degrees of freedom, chi-square was noted to be significant at the 0.05 level with a value at or in excess of 5.99, and at the 0.01 level with a value at or in excess of 9.21. A Somers d correlation coefficient was regarded as being reliably not the product of chance failure at a level of 0.20. Above 0.20, Somers d indicates the predictive power of the association as opposed to its statistical significance.

COMMENTARY

The case study analysis of 10 international strategic alliances built a picture of the motivation behind the formation of those alliances the characteristics the partners had sought in each other, and the manner in which the alliances had fared over time. This illustrated such pitfalls as limiting attitudes and ineffective behaviour, and, more positively, showed the wisdom of flexibility, the vital nature of positive attitudes (including commitment and trust), and the key importance of such issues as congruent objectives, strategic fit and cultural sensitivity. The development of the questionnaire for the 10 case studies enabled the interviews—and follow-ups where necessary—to cover similar ground, and explore some of the same fundamental questions in a more disciplined and consistent fashion than the semistructured interviews.

However, a major interest in strategic alliance research is to gain insights into the most important matters to consider when deciding to form and manage an alliance that has relevance beyond its immediate context. In order to pursue a statistical analysis of responses to the questionnaire, the sample was extended from 10 to 67 cases. Statistical analysis was considered an important addition to qualitative analysis, in order to provide a more rigorous test of the propositions investigated in the first part of the research. The data from the additional cases were obtained from senior executives closely involved in the partner companies of alliances.

Quantitative implications

The quantitative analysis suggested a number of interesting factors. First, it was not possible to associate the selection of the alliance form with the effectiveness of the alliance. More work needs to be done in this area since 67 alliances, when divided into the three categories of joint ventures, collaborations and consortia, give category samples that are too small to permit meaningful conclusions to be drawn. Furthermore, when the question of the selection of the appropriate alliance form was posed in question 9c, 93 per cent answered 'yes', thereby invalidating the question as an effectiveness discriminant.

The identification of strong motivations for alliance formation was generally a poor predictor of alliance effectiveness. The strength of the Resource Dependency Perspective was clearly shown in the frequency tests, but the only motivations significantly associated with success were globalization and economies of scale and/or scope.

Partner selection criteria showed no association with alliance effectiveness, since virtually all alliances claimed at least asset complementarity and potential synergies, yet some were very effective and some less so. Here the limitation of perceptual data revealed itself most powerfully, since, if the claimed complementarities could have been measured more objectively, clear associations with effectiveness may well have been seen.

The management and evolution variables, however, all showed some association with alliance effectiveness at the aggregate variable level, but only certain variables were significant at the normally accepted significance level of 0.05 or better. Of the most significant variables, there were very clear differences in levels of chi-square value, and hence of significance. Thus, positive partner attitudes was the most strongly associated variable, with a chi-square of 23.3, followed some way behind by organizational arrangements (14.1), organizational learning (10.3) and evolution (6.3).

The existence of (a) congruent goals between the partners, (b) balanced benefits, and (c) strong bonding all showed association with alliance effectiveness but at significance levels higher than 0.05. However, congruent goals was significant at the 0.07 level and had a high Somers d value at 0.47, so it was decided to include this variable in the cluster and factor analyses that were subsequently performed.

At the more detailed level of the operational variables, a similar overall picture was revealed, but a number of additional operational variables appeared as significant, when allowed to emerge from the shadows of their aggregate variable. Thus commitment, mutual trust and cultural sensitivity were seen to be the positive attitudes most strongly associated with alliance effectiveness. The organizational arrangements most important to effectiveness were shown to be systems to disseminate information in the partner companies, and a good dispute resolution mechanism.

The variables listed above were then applied to the case-study alliances to establish the level of congruence and possible discrepancy. The findings are presented in Table B.1. As can be seen, the *dynamic* alliances all rated highly on most of the predictive variables. ICL/Fujitsu, Rover/Honda and RBS/Santander were all high on positive attitudes, the most important of all the effectiveness variables. The only caveats were Rover's earlier problems with the Japanese culture, now overcome, and RBS's lower level commitment. Their organizational arrangements are good, with the possible exception of Fujitsu's dispute resolution mechanism. The evolutionary, flexibility, learning and bonding characteristics of all three dynamic alliances are all high. In the case of external drivers, both the Fujitsu and Rover alliances were stimulated by economies of scale and/or scope and by globalization, but RBS/Santander claimed to be motivated by neither of these,

Table B.1 *The statistically significant variables applied to the qualitative case studies*

	Limited			Latent				Dynamic		
	EVC	Imp.	ICI	C&W	Court	D–S	Eur.	RBS	Rover	ICL
External										
Scale/scope	G	G	P	G	A	P	G	P	G	G
Globalization	G	P	A	G	G	P	A	P	G	G
Organizational arrangements	G	A	A	A	A	P	G	G	G	A
Information dissemination	G	G	P	A	A	G	G	G	G	A
Dispute resolution mechanism	G	P	A	A	P	A	G	A	A	P
Positive attitudes										
Top management commitment	A	G	P	G	G	P	G	G	G	G
Lower level commitment	A	G	P	G	G	G	G	G	G	G
Mutual trust	A	G	G	G	G	P	G	P	G	G
Sensitivity to native culture	A	G	P	G	A	P	A	G	I	G
Sensitivity to corporate culture	P	G	P	G	A	P	A	G	I	G
Evolution	A	P	P	A	A	G	A	G	G	G
Flexibility	G	A	P	A	A	G	P	G	G	G
No one partner strategically advantaged	G	G	P	G	A	G	G	G	A	G
Bonded by external challenge	A	P	P	G	P	A	G	G	G	G
Organizational learning	P	P	P	P	P	P	A	G	G	G
Learning dissemination	P	P	P	A	P	P	A	A	G	G
Learning review	P	P	P	P	P	P	P	G	G	G

P = Poor; I = Improving; A = Acceptable; G = Good

but by the threat of regionalization of the European banking market.

In the *latent* category the picture becomes more complex. Eurobrek rates highly on all variables except flexibility, and the willingness to review what it has learned from the alliance. This may well be a useful pointer for future focus within the joint venture and its owners, as elevation to the 'dynamic' category is clearly a future possibility. Dowty–Sema was not set up in response to scale/scope economy opportunities or to the globalization challenge. It rates poorly on lower level commitment, mutual trust, and cultural sensitivity, and although it has evolved dramatically over the period of its existence, this has been more attributable to the winning of larger and larger MOD tenders, than to any internal dynamism. It has not generally shown the qualities of a learning organization. In fact its place in the 'latent' category is largely due to the fact that it is now wholly owned by Bae–Sema, and is in a position to correct these deficiencies. If the venture were to have continued in its 50 per cent two-partner ownership, it is doubtful if it would have left the 'limited' category, despite its good order-winning record. Courtaulds/Nippon Paint also has a mixed profile. While claiming high commitment and trust, it rates no more than acceptable on most other variables, and does not have the advantage of bonding through facing and overcoming an external challenge. It also has low scores on dispute resolution mechanism and organizational learning. Despite the positive attitudes taken within the Courtaulds team, and the longevity of the alliance, on this evidence the alliance needs active attention to become dynamic. Finally, the C&W consortium scores well in most areas. The only major exception is in learning systems where the interviews reveal that the Japanese partners score well but C&W does not. Sensitivity to cultural differences is high, which is vital in a consortium set up in Japan with 23 major Japanese shareholders and led by a UK shareholder without much previous Japanese experience. Given the size of the challenge already overcome, the prognosis for the consortium is good.

The 'limited' category of alliances generally has, as might be expected, the largest number of poor ratings. EVC, however, scores highly on most of the identified criteria, leading to high effectiveness. Only on learning systems, and the partners' sensitivity to culture, is it rated as poor. It is clearly a well-managed joint venture. However, its position in the limited category is largely caused by the facts that (a) it is in the depressed PVC market, (b) it was set up primarily to withdraw capacity in an orderly fashion from the industry, (c) it is reputed to be making large losses in the current recession, and (d) has partners that were thrown together more by circumstance than desire. Its prospects must therefore be limited in its current incarnation. Imperial/Wintermans is also well organized but its limited nature stems from its circumstances. Wintermans is owned by BAT, one of Imperial's major competitors, and Imperial is marketing Wintermans' cigars in the UK alongside, and hence potentially in competition with its own brands. The alliance, therefore, has low scores on evolution, and incidentally also on bonding and learning systems. Continued further evolution seems doubtful. The ICI Pharma alliance is limited in prospects largely because of ICI's attitude towards it. It scores poorly on cultural sensitivity, mutual trust, information dissemination, strategic advantage (Sumitomo is claimed to have taken advantage at ICI's expense), flexibility, bonding and learning systems. In such circumstances, it is perhaps not surprising that ICI are carrying out future development in Japan through other associations.

SUMMARY

This appendix has considered the various factors that stimulate the formation, management and evolution of an alliance, and considered them both in relation to the 10 case studies and to the 67 questionnaire studies. The results have been remarkably consistent. Organizational learning has been judged to be the most important factor in the evolution of an alliance, followed in the qualitative analysis by the adoption by the alliance of new projects and responsibilities. Bonding through successfully surmounting an external challenge has also been perceived as important, and of course complements the development of positive partner attitudes—a positive and developing 'enacted world'. Flexibility and balanced development, although not unimportant, have been consigned to the position of second-order variables from a differentiator of effectiveness viewpoint.

The appendix then considered the overall findings (i.e. not merely those relating to the evolutionary variables) in relation to the case studies, classifying them as dynamic, latent and limited according to the nature of theses findings, and applied the statistically significant variables to the cases in the three categories to discover if this affected the classification. It did not. The quantitative and qualitative findings were judged to be in general broadly consistent with each other, although the quantitative analysis suggested the differential importance of some variables over others—a discriminating exercise more difficult to achieve in the qualitative sample.

References

Achrol, R.V. and Stern, L.W. (1988) 'Environmental determinants of decision-making uncertainty in marketing channels', *Journal of Marketing Research*, 25.

Achrol, R.S., Scheer, L.K. and Stern, L.W. (1990) 'Designing successful transorganizational marketing alliances', Report No. 90–118, Cambridge, MA: Marketing Science Institute.

Aiken, M. and Hage, J. (1968) 'Organizational interdependence intra-organizational structure', *American Sociological Review*, 33, 912–30.

Amit, R. and Schoemaker, P.J.H. (1993) 'Strategic assets and organisational rent', *Strategic Management Journal*, 14, 33–46.

Astley, W.G. (1984) 'Towards an appreciation of collective strategy', *Academy of Management Review*, 9 (3), 526–35.

Axelrod, R. (1984) *The Evolution of Cooperation*. New York: Harper Collins.

Barnard, C.I. (1968) *The Functions of the Executive*. Cambridge, MA: Harvard University Press.

Beamish, R.W. and Banks, J.C. (1987) 'Equity joint ventures and the theory of the multinational enterprise', *Journal of International Business Studies*, Summer, 1–15.

Bertodo, R. (1990) 'The collaboration vortex: anatomy of a Euro-Japanese alliance', *EIU Japanese Motor Business*, Summer, 29–43.

Bleeke, J. and Ernst, D. (1991) 'The way to win in cross-border alliances', *Harvard Business Review*, Nov./Dec., 129–135.

Bresser, R.K. and Harl, J.E. (1986) 'Collective strategy: vice or virtue?', *Academy of Management Review*, 11 (2), 408–27.

Bronder, C. and Pritzl, R. (1992) 'Developing strategic alliances: a conceptual framework for successful cooperation', *European Management Journal*, 10 (4), Dec., 412–20.

Buzzell, R.D. and Gale, B.T. (1987) *The Pims Principle*. New York: Free Press.

Casti, J.L. (1991) *Paradigms Lost*. London: Abacus Books.

Chandler, A.D. (1990) *Scale and Scope: The Dynamics of Industrial Capitalism*. Boston, MA: Harvard University Press.

Cohen, L. and Holliday, M. (1982) *Statistics for Social Scientists*. London: Harper and Row.

Coyne, K.P. (1986) 'Sustainable competitive advantage: what it is, what it isn't', *Business Horizons*, 29 (1).

Garrette, B. and Dussauge, P. (1990) 'Towards an empirically-based taxonomy of strategic alliances between rival firms'. Conference Paper to 10th Annual Conference of SMS, Stockholm.

Geringer, J.M. and Hebert, L. (1989) 'Control and performance of international joint ventures', *Journal of International Business Studies*, Summer, 235–54.

Ghemawat, P., Hamel, G. and Prahalad, V.K. (1986) 'Patterns in international coalition activity', in *Competition in Global Industries* (M.E. Porter, ed.). Boston, MA: Harvard University Press.

Glaister, K.W. and Buckley, P.J. (1994) 'UK international joint venture: an analysis of patterns of activity and distribution', *British Journal of Management*, Feb.

Granovetter, M. (1985) 'Economic action and social structure: the problems of embeddedness', *American Journal of Sociology*, 3, 481–510.

Grant, R.M. (1991) 'The resource-based theory of competitive advantage: implications for strategy formulation', *California Management Review*, Spring, 114–35.

Gupta, A.K. and Singh, H. (1991) 'The governance of synergy: inter-SBU coordination vs external strategic alliances'. Conference Paper to Academy of Management, Miami.

Hamel, G. (1991) 'Competition for competence and inter-partner learning within international strategic alliances', *Strategic Management Journal*, 12, 83–103.

Handy, C. (1992) 'Balancing corporate power: a new federalist paper', *Harvard Business Review*, Nov./Dec., 59–72.

Harrigan, K.R. (1986) *Managing for Joint Venture Success*. Boston, MA: Lexington Books.

Hennart, J.F. (1988) 'A transaction cost theory of equity joint ventures', *Strategic Management Journal*, 9, 361–74.

Hill, C.W.L. (1990) 'Cooperation, opportunism, and the invisible hand: implications for transaction cost theory', *Academy of Management Review*, 15 (3), 500–13.

Johoda, M., Deutsch, M. and Cook, S. W. (1951) *Research Methods in Social Relations*. New York: Dryden Press

Johnson, G. and Scholes, K. (1993) *Exploring Corporate Strategy*, third edition. London: Prentice-Hall.

Kanter, R.M. (1989) *When Giants Learn to Dance*. London: Simon & Schuster.

Killing, J.P. (1983) *Strategies for Joint Venture Success*. Beckenham: Croom Helm.

Killing, J.P. (1988) 'Understanding alliances: the role of task and organisational complexity', in *Cooperative Strategies in International Business* (F.J. Contractor, ed.). Boston, MA: Lexington Books, pp. 55–67.

Kogut, B. (1988) 'Joint ventures: theoretical and empirical perspectives', *Strategic Management Journal*, 9, 319–32.

Kotter, J.P. (1979) 'Managing external dependence', *Academy of Management Review*, 4 (1), 87–92.

Lei, D. and Slocum, J.W. Jr (1991) 'Global strategic alliances; payoffs and pitfalls', *Organizational Dynamics*, 44–62.

Levine and White (1961) 'Exchange as a conceptual framework for the study of inter-organisational relationships', *Administrative Science Quarterly*, March.

Litwak and Hylton (1962) 'Interorganisational analysis—a hypothesis on co-ordinating agencies', *Administrative Science Quarterly*, March.

Lorange, P. and Probst, G.J.B. (1987) 'Joint ventures as self-organising systems: a key to successful joint venture design and implementation', *Columbia Journal of World Business*, Summer, 71–84.

Lorange, P. and Roos, J. (1992) *Strategic Alliances: Formation, Implementation and Evolution*. Oxford: Basil Blackwell.

Lyles, M.A. (1987) 'Common mistakes of joint venture experienced firms', *Columbia Journal of World Business*, Summer, 79–84.

Lynch, R.P. (1990) 'Building alliances to penetrate European markets', *Journal of Business Strategy*, March/April, 4–8.

Mattsson, L.G. (1988) 'Interaction strategies: a network approach'. Working Paper.

McQuitty, L.L. (1957) 'Eliminating linkage analysis from isolating orthogonal and oblique types and typical relevancies', *Journal of Educational Psychology*, 7, 207–29.

Niederkofler, M. (1991) 'The evolution of strategic alliances: opportunities for managerial influence', *Journal of Business Venturing*, 6, 237–57.

Ohmae, K. (1989) 'The global logic of strategic alliances', *Harvard Business Review*, March/April, 143–54.

Osborn, R.N. and Baughn, C.C. (1987) 'New patterns in the formation of US/Japanese cooperative ventures: the role of technology', *Columbia Journal of World Business*, Summer, 57–64.

Pfeffer, J. and Nowak, P. (1976) 'Joint ventures and interorganisational interdependence', *Administrative Science Quarterly*, 21, 398–417.

Pfeffer, J. and Salancik, G. (1978) *The External Control of Organizations*. New York: Harper.

Porter, M.E. (1980) *Competitive Strategy*. New York: The Free Press.

Porter, M.E. (1985) *Competitive Advantage*. New York: The Free Press.

Porter, M.E. and Fuller (1986) 'Coalitions and global strategy', in *Competition in Global Industries* (M.E. Porter, ed.). Cambridge, MA: Harvard University Press.

Powell, W.W. (1990) 'Neither market nor hierarchy: network forms of organisation', *Research in Organisational Behaviour*, 12, 295–336.

Prahalad, C.K. and Hamel, G. (1990) 'The core competence of the corporation', *Harvard Business Review*, 90, 79–91.

Pucik, V. (1988) 'Strategic alliances, organisational learning, and competitive advantage: the HRM agenda', *Human Resource Management*, Spring, 27 (1), 77–93.

Reich, R.B. and Mankin, E.D. (1986) 'Joint ventures with Japan give away our future', *Harvard Business Review*, March/April, 78–86.

Roehl, T.W. and Truitt, J.F. (1987) 'Stormy open marriages are better', *Columbia Journal of World Business*, Summer, 87–95.

Senge, P.M. (1992) *The 5th Discipline: The Art and Practice of the Learning Organization*. London: Century Business.

Snow, C.C. and Hrebiniak, L.G. (1980) 'Strategy, distinctive competence and organizational performance', *Administrative Science Quarterly*, 25, 317–36.

Snyder, A.V. and Ebeling, H.W. (1993) 'Targeting a company's real core competencies', *Journal of Business Strategy*, Winter, 26–32.

Stopford, J.M. and Turner, L. (1985) *Britain and the Multinationals*. Chichester: Wiley.

Taucher, G. (1988) 'Beyond alliances', *IMD Perspectives for Managers*, No. 1.

Teramoto, Y., Kanda, M. and Iwasaki, N. (1991) 'The strategic alliances between Japanese and European companies—cooperative competition, a growth strategy for the 90s'. Research Report No. 91–05.

Thompson, J.D. (1967) *Organizations in Action*. New York: McGraw-Hill.

Thorelli, H.B. (1986) 'Networks: between markets and hierarchies', *Strategic Management Journal*, 7, 37–51.

Index